# THE
# RULES
## OF
# THINKING

# Pearson

At Pearson, we have a simple mission: to help people make more of their lives through learning.

We combine innovative learning technology with trusted content and educational expertise to provide engaging and effective learning experiences that serve people wherever and whenever they are learning.

From classroom to boardroom, our curriculum materials, digital learning tools and testing programmes help to educate millions of people worldwide – more than any other private enterprise.

Every day our work helps learning flourish, and wherever learning flourishes, so do people.

To learn more, please visit us at **www.pearson.com/uk**

# THE
# RULES
## OF
# THINKING

## RICHARD TEMPLAR

# Pearson

Harlow, England • London • New York • Boston • San Francisco • Toronto • Sydney
Dubai • Singapore • Hong Kong • Tokyo • Seoul • Taipei • New Delhi
Cape Town • São Paulo • Mexico City • Madrid • Amsterdam • Munich • Paris • Milan

**PEARSON EDUCATION LIMITED**
KAO Two
KAO Park
Harlow CM17 9SR
United Kingdom
Tel: +44 (0)1279 623623
Web: www.pearson.com/uk

---

**First edition published 2019** (print and electronic)

© Richard Templar 2019 (print and electronic)

ISBN: 978-1-292-26380-9 (print)
      978-1-292-26381-6 (PDF)
      978-1-292-26382-3 (eBook)

**British Library Cataloguing-in-Publication Data**
A catalogue record for the print edition is available from the British Library

**Library of Congress Cataloging-in-Publication Data**
A catalog record for the print edition is available from the Library of Congress

10 9 8 7 6 5 4 3
23 22 21 20 19

Cover design by Nick Redeyoff

Print edition typeset in 11/13, ITC Berkeley Oldstyle Pro by SPi Global
Print edition printed by Bell & Bain

NOTE THAT ANY PAGE CROSS REFERENCES REFER TO THE PRINT EDITION

# Contents

## Thinking creatively  88

## Problem solving  110

## Critical thinking  188

## These are the Rules  220

# Introduction

'I think, therefore I am', as the French philosopher Descartes famously wrote. By which he meant that we know we exist precisely because we have the ability to question whether we exist. All very philosophical, however it underlines the fact that thinking is at the very root of who we are.

So it follows that the more clearly, effectively and coherently we think, the better we are able to live. Happiness and success can flow from good thinking in a way we struggle to achieve if our thought processes are muddled, messy, incoherent. Our thoughts influence our feelings, so it is important to get this foundation right. Once you can think well, you have the basis on which to build the rest of your life.

This is not a book of tips and strategies for thinking. There are lots of those out there, and some of them are very useful, but you won't find many of their techniques here. This book is different – it's about your mindsets, your ways of thinking. It's about understanding why you think as you do and using that insight to improve the way you think. To adapt a traditional saying: 'Give a man a thought and you feed his brain for a day. Teach him how to think, and you feed his brain for life', I want to pass on a lifetime of observations and experience about the kinds of thinking that really work for people. The habits that turn you into a first-class mind. A Rules thinker.

And it is all about habit. We spend all our waking life thinking, so we stop monitoring how we're doing it. We get sloppy without even noticing. When you take your driving test you consciously do everything just as you've learnt it, but by the time you've been driving a few years you're crossing your hands on the steering wheel, slipping the clutch ... you've stopped thinking about it. That's great for all the bits you're still getting right – it's good news that you can now steer instinctively – but when it really matters you've forgotten some of the key skills without even knowing it.

Whether or not we learnt good thinking habits as children, we still need to monitor the way we think. We can learn new skills, brush up the rusty ones, drop the bad habits we've got into. Researchers have recently discovered that it takes a good 66 days to embed a new habit. That's just over two months. It was a proper scientific study with no agenda so there's no reason to doubt its findings,* although of course it's an average figure and doesn't necessarily take into account whether or not the new habit is useful or enjoyable, or whether it's a weekly or an hourly habit, which must make a difference. Still, it's evident that you can learn to think smarter as a matter of course if you practise the Rules for a couple of months or so (there's a section at the end of the book to help you with how to do this). The difference in your life and your work will be apparent as soon as you start, before the 66 days or so that turn it into a habit are up.

It won't all become unconscious after that, though, because as you read the book you'll realise that a lot of the Rules of Thinking are about being conscious of your thought processes. A lot of the problem of messy thinking stems from the fact that we're not aware of how our brains are working and we need to get more of a handle on that if we want to send our thoughts down the right paths. Once this becomes habit, it isn't the effort it might sound like. For one thing, we generally put effort into thinking even when we're doing it badly, so you'll mostly be redirecting the same amount of effort. For another thing, being a Rules thinker doesn't mean you can't ever switch off, have downtime, veg out in front of a screen. Of course you can – your brain needs a rest from time to time, same as your body.

The habit of monitoring your thinking is really about questioning yourself, and observing how your mind is functioning, because of the insights that brings. For example, if you and your partner

---

* These things are important – Rule 93 Don't trust statistics.

argue about whose turn it is to do the dishes, it's easy to wind each other up. Regardless of who actually does the dishes in the end. A Rules thinker questions why they are wound up and asks themselves, 'Why have I just had this argument? What's really happening?' Very few arguments about the dishes are actually about the dishes. They're about feeling taken for granted, or being expected to fit gender roles, or feeling exploited. Until you've thought that through, the dishes might be clean, but you haven't actually addressed the problem. So no surprise then that next time the dishes need doing, the argument will blow up all over again.

Some smarter ways of thinking make you feel happier and more resilient and others help you to organise more effectively or make better decisions. Rules thinking will improve your creativity and your problem-solving skills, and your ability to analyse, evaluate and critique intelligently. Thinking smarter will have a positive impact on every part of your life – at home, at work, in your relationships.

To some extent, this book isn't about how to think at all. Many of the Rules are about how to remove the barriers that get in the way of good, clear thinking. How to avoid self-interest, sidestep assumption, dodge the pitfalls. Once you do that, it's easy to think clearly.

It would be implausibly convenient if there just happened to be exactly 100 Rules of Thinking. So these are the key 100, which are more than enough to change your thought patterns significantly for the better. Once you've mastered these Rules, you'll be much better placed to notice more of your own. Please feel free to share them on my Facebook page, if you'd like to, and help other people join you as a fully fledged Rules thinker.

*Richard Templar*

www.facebook.com/richardtemplar

# Publisher's acknowledgements

**7 René Descartes:** French philosopher: René Descartes (1596-1650) **29 Edward Fitzgerald:** The Rubaiyat of Omar Khayyam (as translated by FitzGerald) **56 Alfred, Lord Tennyson:** Alfred, Lord Tennyson his poem, Ulysses. 1842 **71 Robert J. Hanlon:** Robert J. Hanlon **89 Thomas Edison:** Thomas Edison **92 William Shakespeare:** William Shakespeare **98 Linus Pauling:** Linus Pauling **103 Teena Marie:** "Marry Me", Teena Marie Album Congo Square. **180 Henry Ford:** Henry Ford **190 John Donne:** John Donne

# THINK FOR YOURSELF

If you want to be a top-notch thinker, you have to do the work yourself. That is to say, you have to do the thinking. You can't let anyone else do it for you. That might sound obvious, but you'd be surprised how often we take the convenient shortcut of adopting other people's thinking.

All right, I'll let you off working out the theory of relativity for yourself. There are specialist areas where you don't have the skills to do the relevant thinking, and you're allowed to let scientists, mathematicians, top-flight economists and statisticians and engineers do your thinking for you.* Even so, don't take their word for anything until you've established in your own mind that they know what they're talking about and have no discernible bias.

Other than these exceptions – where you need high-level training to understand the thought processes – from now on, you do all your own thinking, for yourself, by yourself. Unless you're an independent thinker, you really can't call yourself a thinker at all.

Everyone has a different perspective, and another person's logic isn't always going to be right for you. We are all individuals, and not only is it lazy to let other people think for you, it doesn't necessarily lead to the right conclusions. So the Rules in this first section are the foundation that you need to lay before you can get any value from the remaining Rules of Thinking.

---

* Apologies if you're a world-class physicist.

# Avoid echo chambers

When you're a child, you don't know any better than to think as your parents tell you to. If they say it's bad to put your elbows on the table or good to change your underwear every day, you believe them. It's part of being a child to absorb your parents' values and systems. As you get older, you start to find that your teachers have a slightly different set of rules, and your school friends may have values or opinions that are different again. So you start to modify your earlier views and incorporate others that you acquire from fellow students or friends who might think very differently from your parents. And when you're young you probably think about these quite carefully.

Of course, it's easy and comfortable to hang out with other people who broadly think the same way as you. As you form your values, you look for other people who are like-minded. It means you have plenty in common and you don't have endless arguments. When someone else says what you were already thinking, it makes you feel validated, makes you feel you must be right, reinforces your view, makes you feel like you belong. It's a good feeling and you can all spend time together validating each other's beliefs and making yourselves feel right and valued. You can find a partner who thinks the same as you, can have friends like you, can work in a place where there are other people who think the way you do.

And this is what we call an echo chamber. Yes, it's comfortable and affirming, but it makes it very difficult to be your own person. Everyone in your world votes the same way, supports the same causes, has the same beliefs, prejudices and values, and all belong to social media and online groups that reinforce them.

And it gets harder and harder to think in any other way. For one thing, you've virtually cut yourself off from being exposed to different ways of looking at the world, except perhaps so you and your friends can all agree on how wrong they are, in a self-congratulatory way. And that means you don't want to change your views or, presumably, your friends will all agree how wrong *you* are, and that's not going to feel very nice.

And yet, and yet . . . the world is full of people, lots of them lovely people, who don't agree with you about everything. You may rarely encounter them, but can they really all be wrong? Some of them are just as clever as you and have arrived at their beliefs in as valid a way as you have. Maybe more valid – because you've stopped thinking for yourself and moved in to a groupthink where your views are the collective ones, where you don't really ever have to challenge yourself any more. You're no longer an independent person. You've unwittingly become a bit of a sheep.

If you want to be a Rules thinker, you need to change this, shake things up, force yourself to broaden your views, listen to other ideas with a genuine open mind. About the best way to do this is to cultivate friends based on who they are, not what they believe. Aim to have friends of all ages, from other cultures, varied backgrounds, different classes from your own. Between them, they'll make you see the world in a more nuanced way and, if your beliefs can't match up with all of them – because they're not all the same – you'll have to think for yourself.

> ## CULTIVATE FRIENDS BASED ON WHO THEY ARE, NOT WHAT THEY BELIEVE

# RULE 2

# Don't be scared

It can be frightening to start thinking for yourself. Who knows where it could lead? You could end up with any number of principles and beliefs that don't sit comfortably with the people you spend your time with. You could find yourself out on a limb. You could have to face up to realising you've been wrong about things, or at least not been right about them. One of the barriers to being an independent thinker is the fear of being different.

Look, that's understandable, of course it is. But you can take things gently. There are no thought police out there – not yet anyway. No one else has to know what you're thinking until you're ready to let on. You don't have to sit your whole family down and say, 'I need you all to know that I think your way of life is wrong and I entirely reject it.' Thinking for yourself doesn't entail sharing your new beliefs until you want it to.

If you start to cultivate friends with different backgrounds and beliefs, this all gets much easier – just one of the upsides of doing it. Once you step out of the echo chamber, having independent thoughts is much more readily accepted and you'll have the fun of meeting people who agree with your new thoughts and people who don't – both equally interesting and enjoyable. You have to accept other people's differences too, of course, and not feel threatened by them. Listen to them and then make up your own mind.

If you're used to agreeing with everyone around you, of course it can be quite daunting to say that you don't share their views. So wait until you're ready before you say it and then be prepared for them to feel threatened by you. How you handle this is up to you, but you'll be much happier about your choice if you've thought it through in advance. I'd add that, if you respect their view, they are more likely to respect yours, and that's as it should be. I've observed, unsurprisingly, that people who respect others' views, even when they don't share them, are more popular than those who can't accept difference.

When you think for yourself, it's not only about ideas and values and politics and religion. You need to think for yourself at work and in practical matters too. If you're working alongside other people it can be scary the first time you say, 'I think there's a better way to do things.' But give it a go – keep it practical, respectful and non-critical and you should find you get a positive response. If you've done your thinking carefully, you're probably right and people will appreciate that. If they persuade you that your ideas aren't as good as you think, don't take it personally, but keep thinking for yourself and analyse their comments – maybe they're right. So hone your thinking skills for next time, but don't be put off. All independent thinkers need a bit of courage – look at Galileo or Darwin – but it only takes your colleagues to say, 'That's a great idea!' for you to feel inspired to voice your thoughts again next time.

IF YOU RESPECT THEIR VIEW,
THEY ARE MORE LIKELY TO
RESPECT YOURS

# RULE 3

# Consider the motive

Some people are more persuasive than others. Whether they're trying to sell you a car, persuade you to adopt their plan at work, convince you to come to their party, or point out why plastic bags are bad for the environment. You need to avoid being sucked into following their line of thought blindly without engaging your own brain.

Now, that car might not be what you need at all. On the other hand, plastic bags really are bad for the environment. So if someone wants you to adopt their belief or follow their advice, you can't deduce from that alone whether it's a good idea. You have to know why they're seeking to persuade you.

It's always a good idea to understand what this person wants you to believe and why. Sometimes they want you to do something as a result of their persuasive efforts – buy something, join something, agree to something, attend an event, sign a petition. Not always though. Sometimes they're simply passing on an opinion and would like your agreement – maybe they want to persuade you it's a good thing the council are building a new car park. It's a nice bonding feeling when someone agrees with you, but beyond that they may not be after much at all.

Once you've established clearly in your mind what they want, it's much easier to decide whether you want it too. Your friend is telling you how great the party will be because they want you to go. They're only guessing it will be great. Do you agree? Do you want to be there? If so, do you want to be there because it will be great or because you want to support your friend? It's much easier to inure yourself to your friend's persuasive methods once you can see them for what they are.

Of course, that might be the perfect car for you, whatever the salesperson's motive for telling you so. You can't dismiss it out of hand just because they have a vested interest in you buying it (if that ruled it out, no one would ever buy a car from any dealer). Identifying the motive isn't a reason to reject someone else's thinking. The point of doing it is to give yourself a sensible dose of wariness, of where you should double-check their assertions and make sure their arguments are the ones that matter.

A car salesperson might get you really excited with their infectious enthusiasm about how fast this car is or how comfortable it is in the back seats, but don't get swept along mindlessly. Are those things actually important to you? Your colleague might persuade you that this exhibition is just the way to reach all those small engineering businesses out there. But how big a proportion of your customers are they ever going to be? So why does your colleague care so much about reaching them? Only by recognising the motive can you know how much importance to attach to the facts you're being fed.

# IDENTIFYING THE MOTIVE ISN'T A REASON TO REJECT SOMEONE ELSE'S THINKING

# RULE 4

# Beware self-interest

Never mind other people's motives for a moment – what about your own? What do you stand to gain from thinking as you do? It's easy to think in a way that feeds your own self-interest without ever being aware that you're doing it. It's possible that your way of thinking will lead you to a decision that will make you better off financially, or give you higher status, or enable you to live in a better area. This is something that I notice often affects politicians, who are very good at thinking in a way that is likely to get them re-elected. Most of them find it quite hard to reach conclusions that won't sit comfortably with the voters.

We've all met vegetarians who stopped eating meat because of their ethical views, who have somehow managed to justify revising those views when they discover how much they miss meat. No, I'm not knocking it, I'm one of them myself. The answer is not necessarily to revert to vegetarianism, just to be more honest with yourself about why you don't.

However, the self-interested way of thinking isn't always so tangible. I spoke to someone recently who applied for a job he really wanted and didn't get it. He asked for feedback and, initially, took it on board. But after he'd had a while to dwell on it, he slowly came around to thinking that the feedback was unfair and the interviewers were at fault for failing to see his strengths. Now actually, as you and I know, it isn't the interviewers' responsibility to search for the qualities they want – it's the candidate's responsibility to demonstrate them. But this chap wanted it to be the interviewers' fault he didn't get the job, because that soothed his ego, so he thought about it in a way that convinced him he was the best candidate. Of course, the problem with this is that he hasn't learnt anything for next time, so presumably he's less likely to get the next job he applies for.

You've got to be honest with yourself and you won't always like it. If the unsuccessful interviewee wants to think truthfully, he'll have to accept that either he wasn't right for the job or, if he was, he failed to show it.

Self-esteem is a big part of what tempts us to skew our thinking to suit our purposes. Envy is another and is often related to self-esteem. Easier to think your colleague got that lucrative account because the boss favours them, than because they might actually be able to handle it better than you. And, again, you won't get the next big account either if you go down this path, because it blocks you from recognising the need to improve.

If you're a people-pleaser, that opens up huge scope for cover-up thinking. Most of us want to please at least a few people and, if you think the boss would prefer you to agree with them, or you'll fit into your friendship group better if you share their views, there's a motive to fix your conclusion before you've thought it through, and then retro-fit your thinking process to suit. Great for keeping in with people (at least in your own mind), not so good for becoming an independent thinker.

> # SELF-ESTEEM IS A BIG PART OF WHAT TEMPTS US TO SKEW OUR THINKING

# Keep hold of your heartstrings

If you're serious about resisting other people's manipulations and thinking for yourself, it helps to be alert to how they're trying to influence you. If you can spot it, it's much easier to resist. So next time someone seeks to persuade, convince, cajole you round to their perspective, think about the strategies they're using. Generally speaking, they'll use emotion rather than logic. Your job, as a clear thinker, is to resist.

From the other person's perspective, empathy is a good starting point. If someone can convince you that you both *feel* the same way, it seems like a much shorter step to *thinking* the same way. So a natural persuader will try to convince you that you're both coming from the same point. They'll emphasise similarities in your situation or values. They'll tell you they know what it's like to have kids, or work in an office, or struggle to pay the rent, or enjoy buying clothes, or own a cat. The shared experience puts you both in the same place, so now they can metaphorically take you by the hand and lead you to the conclusion they've chosen. Listen to them, but don't let them lead you blindly. Question the route and the destination to be sure it's really where you want to go.

If they can get you emotionally engaged, they will. For one thing, emotion is a powerful force, so they'll want to get you angry about the injustice they're campaigning against, or excited about the clothes they want to sell you, or anxious at the idea of overstretching your budget. And for another thing, it's much harder for you to think rationally once you start to become emotional. So the higher they can crank up your emotions, the more you shut down your rational response to what they're saying. Aim to resist the emotional response so your thinking stays rational and measured. You'll be a much better judge of how valid their point is.

Another favourite ploy is to use weighted words. This can be more insidious and subtle, and tends to work at an unconscious level. We all do it – yes, you too – and it's wise to recognise it in yourself. There's more than one way to describe most things, and the adjectives you use can be powerful. Suppose you read two newspaper descriptions of the same politician. If the papers are from opposite ends of the political spectrum, they're inclined to use different words to depict them. One might describe them as brave while the other says they're foolhardy – both descriptions of the same thing, but they give a very different impression. Is the politician firm or hardline? Are they socially aware or woolly? These word choices can build up to create a persuasive picture that suits the person (or newspaper) in question. I'm always interested in how the media decide who to describe as terrorists, who are rebels, who are freedom fighters, who are resistance forces. Often the only difference between these terms is the way the person using them wants you to respond. So notice the word choices the other person is making and substitute your own, neutral words in your head so you can think more clearly.

Bear in mind that, consciously or unconsciously, you employ these same techniques yourself when you want to persuade someone else. So not everyone who tries to convert you to their way of thinking is knowingly manipulating or tricking you. Whether you agree with them or not, they're entitled to hold their view and they're entitled to express it. And you are entitled to resist it, or not, once you've thought it through rationally for yourself.

> # IF YOU CAN SPOT IT, IT'S MUCH EASIER TO RESIST

# Don't be gullible

If you believe everything I've told you so far, just because it's written down in black and white, then think again. Yes, *I* believe it all, but you should be thinking it through for yourself. How do you know you can trust me? You've never met me, you don't know who I am, you don't even know what I look like. Just because I've had a book published doesn't mean I know everything.

Look, you can't go through life never trusting anyone, but neither is it helpful to be too trusting. And the best insurance against going too far either way is to think for yourself. So thank you for buying (or borrowing) my book and please feel free to read it. I hope you'll find, when you think it through, that it makes enough sense that you don't consider your time or your money wasted. But don't believe everything I write just because I've written it.

I've talked about how to recognise the ways people might prod you into thinking their way instead of your own. But there will always be people who come up with new and clever strategies or people who know you so well they can find your weak spot instinctively. The thing is, if you can make your own decisions for yourself, you don't need to trust or mistrust other people. It doesn't matter, because you're not in their hands, you're in your own. Of course there are other scenarios where trust might be an issue but, when it comes to persuasion, thinking for yourself is the trump card that sidesteps it.

One way to avoid being gullible is always to give yourself time to think, since thinking is the solution. Never allow anyone to force you into a faster decision than you're happy with. Too much pressure is usually a sign that they're worried you'll change your mind if you have time to think. You know those special one-day-only offers – sign your name here today and you'll get a big discount or a free thing. My absolute rule is that I never trust that kind of offer and I rarely trust the assertion that the offer won't still be there if I go back tomorrow.

I never trust a bargain either, until I've thought it through. If I want the thing anyway, it's just a bonus that it's so well priced. If I don't really want it, even a few pence for it would be a few pence wasted.

Oh, one other thing to think about . . . charities, while largely worthy causes, do know every trick in the book when it comes to getting money off you. And their armoury also includes guilt, whether overt or implied. Now I'm a big believer in giving to charities, but all of us have only so much we can afford to give to charity each year. So think through the charities you really want to support – wildlife, army veterans, old people, children, the environment – and give that money to them, whether it's a regular subscription or an occasional donation. Don't be sucked into giving that money to other charities just because someone shakes a tin in your face and makes you feel guilty. If it's any more than a handful of loose change, go away, and think about whether you want to support them. You can always make a donation online or come back tomorrow. If you think that's harsh, no problem. At least you're thinking.

> ## DON'T BELIEVE EVERYTHING I WRITE JUST BECAUSE I'VE WRITTEN IT

# RESILIENT THINKING

One of the absolute foundations of healthy thinking is resilience. Some of us start out naturally more resilient than others, but the good news is we all have some resilience to begin with. And the even better news is you can teach yourself to be more resilient by training your mind to think in the right way.

Let's just establish exactly what resilience is. The more resilient you are, the faster and better you will bounce back from anything bad, negative, traumatising. Most of us can come to terms with missing the bus, but not everyone recovers well from bereavement or abuse or redundancy or serious illness. Of course they don't, but it's still the case that some people cope better than others. So what are they doing that means they're able to come to terms with life's tragedies?

Resilient people have higher levels of belief in themselves and their power to control their own lives. This gives them confidence that they will overcome their difficulties in time.

In my experience, the people who cope best with disaster are usually the same ones who cope best with missing the bus. That's really useful because it means you can practise being resilient every time you miss the bus, or burn the food, or have a bad cold, or can't afford a new item of clothing you fancy. Once you believe you can cope with the little things, it gets easier to believe in your ability to cope with the bigger things when they come along. So let's look at the kinds of thinking that will make you a more resilient person.

# Know who you are

A friend of mine was diagnosed with a very serious illness. Of course people kept asking her how she was, what was happening with the treatment, what she was and wasn't able to do and how could they help. She found this very frustrating and in the end she sent round an email to everyone saying that she really appreciated their concern and their offers of help, but she didn't want to talk about it thank you. She explained to me that it wasn't that she actually minded talking about the illness per se, it was that she felt she was starting to be defined by it.

Now this particular friend of mine is amazingly resilient and had an instinctive recognition that in order to cope with her diagnosis she had to separate it from her own identity. She had to go on being the same person she was before she became ill and, for her, that meant discouraging other people from talking about it. She didn't want her friends to see her only in terms of her illness, because – more importantly – she didn't want to get sucked into seeing herself the same way. She had several important roles in life – at work, as a mother, as a partner, as a friend – and those were the ones she liked and had created for herself. So those were the things she wanted people to see when they thought about her. By drawing these lines firmly around herself, she was separating her own identity from that of the illness.

This is central to being resilient, coping with stress, enabling yourself to overcome hardship. A lot of us muddle the bound-aries between ourselves and our problems. Once you recognise that this is making it harder for you to cope, you can focus on thinking about your situation differently. You don't have to adopt my friend's strategy of asking people not to talk about it, but it's a useful tactic for some. One friend whose husband died refused to use the word 'widow' because it described her situation and not herself.

This is crucial when you're coping with serious illness or bereavement, and it's essential when you've had a serious blow to your self-esteem that you're tempted to see as a rejection of some kind. Redundancy, for example, or a relationship break-up. If you see these as a direct criticism of everything you are, then you call into question your entire identity and indeed your value as a person. Redundancy might have nothing whatever to do with your value as an employee and, if you personalise it, you give your self-confidence an unnecessarily tough mountain to climb. You've got enough on your plate finding a new job without the added stress of feeling you're a failure.

A relationship break-up or not getting a job you're after is not a reflection of your entire self. Think about all the aspects of yourself that it doesn't relate to – the rest of your life, your friends, your values, your skills, your strengths. If you and your partner split up it doesn't mean that you're a failure, it simply means that the relationship didn't work. Yes, I know it's hard to see it like that at times, but you have to keep reminding yourself that you are still the same you, and this is only one aspect of your life. However much your relationship means to you, it isn't actually who you are. This way of thinking, this separation of yourself from your troubles, is going to make it so much less difficult to cope.

> # IF YOU PERSONALISE IT, YOU GIVE YOUR SELF-CONFIDENCE AN UNNECESSARILY TOUGH MOUNTAIN TO CLIMB

# RULE 8

## Seek out support

The resilient among us are much more likely to be surrounded by a good support network. This may or may not include professional help but will certainly involve friends or family who genuinely want to help you overcome your problems. That's not enough in itself though – they have to be reasonably good at it. Some people, bless 'em, are always saying the wrong thing even when they're trying to help. However much of a friend these people are when things are going well, make life easier for yourself by quietly steering clear of them when times are tough. Think about which friends you want around you and which you don't.

And think about the kind of help you need. Support from friends isn't something you just have to suck up. If it isn't helping, it's not actually support in any useful sense and you don't have to accept it. You've got enough on your plate without having to absorb negative input just because it's well meant. You don't have to tell people to their face, 'I don't want your so-called help.' You can just politely turn down invitations to meet up until things are better or, even – and here's a ploy I've used many times – not tell them about the scenario in the first place. Tricky with some problems but easy with others. If you know they'll make you feel worse if you don't get a particular job, think ahead and don't even tell them you've applied for it.

So who are you going to give a bit of a wider berth to when things are going badly? Well, you'd be best off avoiding anyone who is negative, who revels in doom and gloom, who keeps banging on about all the things that could make your problems even worse (although they probably won't). You want positive people around you.

Although not so positive that they keep telling you your feelings are wrong. You know the type: 'It's fine! Stop worrying!' You want empathy, not denial. If anyone behaves like this, refuse to feel bad.

Listen, anyone whose response makes you feel worse is not a good support. Make a mental note for next time. If they don't make you feel better, even if only a little bit, that's them, not you.

Avoid people who try to solve your problems for you too, either by supplying a solution, making a decision on your behalf, or actually enacting it themselves. This is not helpful and will not improve your resilience. It gives you the subconscious message that you can't think or act for yourself. That's not true and it's exactly the belief you are trying to avoid. You value input, but you can make your own decisions and run your own life thank you.

Once you think about what you need and who can provide it, it's much easier to surround yourself with genuinely supportive people when you're in trouble. And tell them what you need – do you want someone to help with the kids and take the pressure off? Someone simply to listen? Someone who can help you with daunting paperwork? Someone to cook you some meals to stick in the freezer? People who genuinely want to help – and you know this from your own experience as a supportive friend – want to know the best way to do just that.

> **YOU CAN MAKE YOUR OWN DECISIONS AND RUN YOUR OWN LIFE THANK YOU**

# Take control

When it comes to interpreting what happens in your life, people fall broadly into two camps. Those who believe that it's all down to fate and you can't change it, and those who believe that you have free will and control your own life. Science has not yet agreed which is the case, but it has established that people who believe they control their own lives tend to be happier.

Believing you control your life is crucial to resilience as well. Apart from anything else it motivates you to find ways of coping or at least new ways to think about your problems even where there's little you can do on the face of it. You can't bring back someone who has died, but if you believe your thinking and your decisions will influence the way you deal with it, you're more likely to try to find remedies.

Some people go on quite strict specialist diets when they have a significant illness. You might think it looks like a quack diet and there's no evidence it will make the slightest difference (although of course you're too polite to say so). You might even be right – or you might not. It really doesn't matter. What matters is that by taking control so dramatically, these people are improving their own resilience. So to that degree at least their diet is definitely beneficial.

What's the alternative to taking control? Well, if you feel everything in life is fated and you can do nothing about it, you are painting yourself as a victim when things go badly. And feeling like a victim takes power away from you and leaves you helpless. It does nothing for your confidence and your ability to bounce back.

When things go badly, do something about it. If you can't directly influence events, take control of your response to them. Think differently, choose who you ask for support and how, practise mindfulness or yoga or go for long walks, take some time out – it doesn't matter which of these you do. The thing that really helps is that you are consciously taking charge of your life.

Obviously if there are practical actions you can take that will help, that's great. Your resilience will improve simply because you're in control. So start looking for another job, or lodge a complaint, or get professional advice, or change your diet, or whatever you can think of that will help. It's a double bonus because both the action, and the fact you're taking it, are good for you. You can be as creative as you like. If you think painting your bathroom blue will make you feel calmer, then paint it blue. I know someone who was struggling so much with a job he hated that he left before he became any more miserable. He couldn't find a job immediately so, instead of feeling sorry for himself, he used the time to do the writing he'd always promised himself he would. He never did find another job because his writing career took off instead.

> ## PEOPLE WHO BELIEVE THEY CONTROL THEIR OWN LIVES TEND TO BE HAPPIER

# Be flexible

Why do engineers use steel and not iron as a structural frame for buildings? Iron is really strong, after all. But steel has one crucial advantage – it's flexible. It doesn't snap because it can bend. Indeed it can be quite disconcerting being at the top of a tall building as it sways in a high wind, but that swaying is the reason it doesn't break. Steel, you see, is resilient.

In scientific terms, resilience in materials means their ability to spring back into shape, their elasticity. And we're no different – we need a degree of elasticity to help us to bounce back in the face of adversity or high winds.

When you're buffeted by metaphorical storms, you have to have a bit of give. You might think that standing firm and giving no ground is the best approach but, if it doesn't work, your ability to recover will suffer. Suppose you've set your heart on buying a particular house. You've been saving up for a deposit for years and you've found the house of your dreams, your offer has been accepted and you've started planning it all out in your head – how you'll use each room, where your furniture will go, how you'll decorate. And then – disaster – the sale falls through. Maybe the chain breaks, or your own buyer pulls out, or you get gazumped.

How you cope with the fallout from this will be down to how resilient you are. Almost anyone will find this stressful, but how stressful and how long before you recover? If you can't imagine any other house but that one, you'll be more stressed and take far longer to get over it than you will if you are flexible enough to recognise there are other options. Either way, you're going to end up somewhere other than this dream house. The only difference is how you adapt to that idea. The more elasticity there is in your thinking, the sooner you'll be out there househunting again, getting excited about a new house, and the quicker you'll finally be ensconced in a lovely new home.

This is a skill you can practise frequently on smaller issues, ones that are frustrating rather than devastating. You've planned a lovely meal out with friends and then discover at the last minute that the restaurant you wanted to go to is closed. Do you get upset or do you think 'Hey, it's the people that matter, let's eat elsewhere, or stay in, or go to the movies'? Next time the shop has sold out of the item you wanted, or you just miss the train, or you come down with a bug just as you arrive on holiday, think flexibly and be prepared to adapt. What have you got to lose? If you can take the minor upsets in your stride by rewriting the script a little bit, you'll be far better placed to do the same thing when life's big dramas come along.

> **RESILIENCE IN MATERIALS MEANS THEIR ABILITY TO SPRING BACK INTO SHAPE, THEIR ELASTICITY**

# Be self-aware

However bad an experience you're going through, you can always learn from it. If you don't, why would things change? If they're bad this time, they'll be bad next time. I spoke to someone recently whose partner had just died. She had had a tough life, having lost her mother at the age of 15. She told me that she'd coped really badly with that and was messed up for a long time. So this time she wasn't going to make the same mistakes again. Now that's resilience.

Think about the things that have gone badly in your life in the past and reflect on how you dealt with them. When new traumas come along, think about how you can handle them. If you keep approaching everything in the same way, you'll keep getting the same results. So stop it and try something new. Think about what has worked in the past, what hasn't, and how you can change.

Did you bottle things up and try to cope on your own last time? Well, if that didn't work I'd recommend a new approach this time – talk to people and ask for support. Did you immerse yourself in work? Did that work? If not, there's no point repeating it.

It's not only about your coping mechanisms, it's the practical things too. If your relationship is breaking down, what can you learn from past experience? Should you talk more? Shout less? Stop working so late every evening? If you clashed badly with your oldest child when they reached adolescence, could you maybe try a different tactic with your next child? If you don't, you run a high risk of hitting all the same problems again. One friend always shouted at her kids for lounging on the floor to watch TV, instead of sitting in the chairs. One day her son asked her why and it stopped her in her tracks. She thought for a moment and realised she couldn't think of a reason – she was just repeating what her parents told her. So she laughed and told him he was right and he could stay where he was. A small thing, but it improved their relationship significantly.

When I was in my twenties, a friend of mine in his sixties told me that you don't stop making mistakes as you get older, but you do find yourself making fresh ones. He said that he ever more frequently found himself thinking, 'Ah, I've tried this before and it definitely didn't work, so I'll try something else this time.' Sometimes it worked, and even when it didn't it was at least interesting. The depressing thing is how many people I know who couldn't say this as they grow older, because in fact they just keep repeating the same old mistakes again and again, wondering why things never seem to get any better.

Know yourself. Know your weak spots, know what helps you, know the things that you can and can't cope with easily, know which potentially negative emotions you're prone to – anger, depression, self-pity, impulsiveness. The better you understand your own psyche, the better prepared you are to face up to hardship and to bounce back swiftly.

> # THE BETTER YOU UNDERSTAND YOUR OWN PSYCHE, THE BETTER PREPARED YOU ARE

# It is what it is

When I have a stinking cold or a nasty bug, I confess I have a bit of a tendency to mention it.* Negatively, apparently. Well I'm not going to be positive about it, am I? However I really must learn to stop doing it. Not because it irritates other people, although I'm told that's a thing, but because it makes me feel worse. Every time I mention it, it reminds me how rubbish I feel. I hear myself saying words like 'I've felt better' or 'Pretty rough actually, since you ask', and ping! I feel pretty rough. What a surprise.

My mother-in-law, who is beyond stoical, takes the opposite approach. When asked how her cold is, I've actually heard her reply, 'What cold?' She'll insist she's fine. The striking thing here, and the reason I must change my habits, is that she copes way better than I do with a cold. She either ignores it completely or tells anyone who asks that she's fine. That's what she hears herself saying, so that's how she feels.

This is the kind of acceptance that builds resilience. She is much more resilient than I am in the face of colds which is, I admit, my loss. When you're facing a much bigger challenge than the common cold, it's even more important. Acceptance is not about giving up.

It's not that my mother-in-law doesn't ever buy a box of tissues or make herself a hot honey and lemon drink. She'll do things to help herself. But if she ran out of lemons it would only be a minor irritation because she's telling herself she doesn't really need it anyway. The important thing is that she accepts she has a cold, she does what she can and she lets go of the rest of it. Railing, moaning, fighting, bitching, don't help. The cold will be there until it has run its course and she lives with that.

---

* It's been said I do this with a mere sniffle, but I deny it.

You can't deal with a challenge until you recognise it. If, in your mind, you're trying to change the inevitable, fight the unbeatable, you're stuck in that place. That's a pain if it's a cold and agonising if it's something far more serious. Sure, change things when you can, but a lot of bad stuff can't be changed. It's unavoidable or it's already in the past. In that case sooner or later you have to accept it before you can move to stage two. The one thing you do have some control over is how soon you do this. I often remind myself of the lines in the *Rubaiyat of Omar Khayyam* (as translated by FitzGerald):

'The moving finger writes; and, having writ,
Moves on: nor all thy piety nor wit
Shall lure it back to cancel half a line,
Nor all thy tears wash out a word of it.'

You could see this as depressing I suppose, but I've always found it deeply reassuring, as I'm certain it was intended to be. It's a waste of effort fighting so you might as well join the moving finger and move on.

## ACCEPTANCE IS NOT ABOUT GIVING UP

# RULE 13

# Don't get over-distracted

'Don't dwell on it,' people say when you're going through tough times. The idea is that it's bad enough as it is, without focusing your mind on it all the time. Better to distract yourself if thinking won't change anything.

There's a lot of sense in this. It's hard to be positive and feel resilient when you're wallowing in misery. A break from thinking about it, maybe some fresh air or just time with friends, is a sensible idea. You want to minimise the stress you're going through, so it makes sense that any stress-reducing activity will help.

There is a 'but', though. Give yourself a break, yes, but don't play hide and seek with your troubles. If you try to run away from them, you solve nothing right now and you pile up stress in the future. Being in denial can work well in small doses – I often think it's quite an underrated strategy – but it's not good for you in the long term. If you think about it that has to make sense because, as long as you're in denial, you can't adopt many of the ways of thinking that will help you to be more resilient. You can't reflect, ask for support, take control of your life, be self-aware, if you're not admitting what's happening to you. Most important of all, as I've said before, you'll never learn to accept a situation you don't admit it exists.

How can you tell which distraction is good and which is bad? It's less about the type of distraction than about the degree. Having said that, activities such as drugs, alcohol, overeating, risky behaviour are best avoided at normal times, and especially when you're using them to hide from your feelings. It's fine to watch TV or play computer games, so long as it's occasional and not a way to block out your thoughts completely.

So it's not what you do, it's why you do it. If you need a bit of a break, that's fine. Carry on. If what you're doing is a displacement activity, it's not healthy. Or at least be aware of it and keep it to a minimum. I make a cup of tea every morning before I start work. I do it only to delay settling down at my desk. However I'm self-aware enough to recognise this, it takes only five minutes, and anyway it helps keep my fluid levels up. There's nothing wrong with indulging this kind of brief displacement activity. The problems come when you spend half your day doing them in order to pretend your life isn't happening.

You need to find some time to reflect, to understand your situation, to think about what you can do to take control of your life and to find acceptance of the things you can't change. You need to learn not to be afraid of being alone with your thoughts. I'm not giving you orders – I just want you to be able to recover as quickly as you can and this is the only way to do it, daunting as it might seem at first.

---

## DON'T PLAY HIDE AND SEEK
## WITH YOUR TROUBLES

---

# Like yourself

There's a strong correlation between resilience and self-esteem. If you like yourself, you'll cope better with adversity than if you don't. So everything that you can do to build your self-esteem now will make you more resilient when trouble strikes.

Self-esteem is about how much worth you believe you have as a person. It's not the same thing as confidence – which is more to do with the skills and abilities you feel you have. This is about the big stuff, about whether you believe you have intrinsic value.

If your self-esteem is low, you will focus on those qualities in yourself that you believe are negative: 'I'm a rubbish friend', 'I'm always getting things wrong', 'I'm stupid, boring, useless . . . ' If you tell yourself, 'I'm *always* selfish', that's a clear sign your self-esteem is low. If any of these opinions of yourself are things you were told as a child, the low self-esteem will be even more entrenched.

Look, I can't raise your self-esteem in a couple of pages of text. I wish I could. You'll notice however that it is called *self*-esteem for a reason. It's no kind of measure of your actual worth, it's just the way you see it. So only you can change it.

We're talking about a spectrum here. Your self-esteem may be up towards the higher end, which is great (you wouldn't want it too high, which is where you find afflictions such as narcissism). But within reason, any improvement will improve your resilience too. If your self-esteem is low, please believe me that it's not a true reflection of your value as a human being, and seek out ways to help yourself match your perception more accurately to the truth.

So change the way you think. Stop comparing yourself with other people, or with some kind of image in your head of what you 'should' be like. You 'should' be you. So don't focus on the standards you think you can't meet. Instead look for the positive. At least once a day, consciously remember all the positive things you've done, whether large or small. All the times you've been kind, all the goals you've achieved. Deny headspace to any negative thoughts. So if you walked four miles, tell yourself, 'I walked four miles!' Do *not* even think about how many more miles you didn't walk. Four is good.

Don't look at what someone else can do and berate yourself for not doing it too. If it's important, resolve to work towards it (at your own speed, not anyone else's). If it's not, who cares what they can do? Bet they can't cook as well as you, or play football, or organise stuff, or fix a puncture, or comfort a crying child. There's a whole picture here. If we compared each thing we could do with one person who could do it brilliantly, we'd all have a worryingly low sense of self-worth. But everyone has their own mix and none of us can do everything.

Finally, surround yourself with people who will reinforce your positive thoughts and avoid anyone who is inclined to tell you you're not good enough. Their opinion probably isn't true and it certainly isn't helpful.

> IT'S NO KIND OF MEASURE OF
> YOUR ACTUAL WORTH, IT'S
> JUST THE WAY YOU SEE IT

# Be ready to cope

There are lots of coping mechanisms that will help when you hit hard times. They will make it easier for you to bounce back from whatever hits you – in other words they will enable you to be more resilient, which is what we want.

If you've just found out that your father is terminally ill, or you've had another miscarriage, or your partner has gambled away your savings, or you haven't got the grades you need, or your child needs a major operation, or your new boss is a nightmare – this is probably not going to feel like a good moment to start learning lots of new skills. And yet there are plenty of skills – some we've covered, some we'll get to in a bit – that will really help you cope.

So the answer is to make sure those skills are up your sleeve just waiting for a moment such as this. You'll have found out what works for you and practised it every time you've missed the bus, or had to deal with your critical mother, or traipsed into work with a stinky cold.

You'll use some of these new thinking habits constantly whether things are good or bad. Others will be strategies you bring into play when you recognise you need to give yourself a bit of a leg-up to cope with things. You'll need these skills polished and ready to go so when things really hit the fan, you can switch them on effortlessly. Because effort isn't going to come easily at those moments.

There are new ways of thinking in the next section (Healthy thinking) which will be really useful to you, so long as you've made habits of them. Oh, they'll have helped even when things were going smoothly, but now you'll really reap the benefits. And there are other strategies too which you'll need to work out for yourself. They're not difficult, but some are new skills worth learning before you need them: yoga, sport, meditation, going for a bike ride, taking a long soaking bath, going out with friends, playing with the dog/cat/budgerigar. Not all of them require training, but you do need to know which are the ones that help you. If you don't have a broad repertoire to cover all moods, weathers, time windows, locations, build up a wider range. If all your coping strategies require you to be at home, for example, think of a useful habit you can develop for when you're at work. Or with the kids. Or when it's snowing.

And it's not enough just to have these personalised tactics ready. You have to recognise when to deploy them. You have to be in the habit of thinking, 'It's been a tough day, I think I'll go for a run' or 'I'm feeling a bit overwhelmed, I'll meditate for 20 minutes when the kids are in bed'. Know what your strategies are, when you need them, and which ones help when.

> ## YOU'LL NEED THESE SKILLS POLISHED AND READY TO GO

# RULE 16

# Better out than in

In the midst of a crisis, you often find that your head is crammed with thoughts, feelings, worries, stress. You can't see where to begin coping because your thoughts are swirling about so fast and erratically that you can't catch them. You're overwhelmed.

One of the most helpful things you can do at this point is to get your thoughts out of your head and on to paper. Research has shown that people who are able to do this report that they feel less stressed afterwards – in other words they can rebound faster from the trauma.

Part of the problem with coping is that you can't get your thoughts to keep still. But they stay still on paper. Whether you splurge it all out at once, or whether you want to go back and re-order it later, you can stop carrying the thoughts and feelings round in your head once you have them safely recorded elsewhere. You don't have to show them to anyone – that's up to you.

Maybe there are things you don't want to forget. You can write down everything you loved about someone who has died and keep adding to it whenever you think of something new. That removes the anxiety that over time you won't remember the important things.

If someone else seems to be the cause of your problems, you can write them a letter – maybe the boss who didn't promote you or the partner who left you. I'm not necessarily advocating posting the letter – that's a different question entirely – but getting your feelings down on paper can be hugely cathartic. I would always advise doing this on paper simply because emails are dangerous. It's so easy to hit 'send' in an unguarded moment and regret it afterwards. No, much better to do it the old-fashioned way on paper. And then wait at least 24 hours before re-reading it. Only then should you send it, if you still feel the need. If you're not certain, wait another 24 hours. And another. Before you put it in the post, think about what the effect will be and how this will help. No point sending it if it won't make you feel better in the long run.

There are lots of ways to get your thoughts clearer on paper. For some people, writing poetry helps. For more prosaic problems, there are more practical ways to put your thinking in order. If you have major financial problems, perhaps a budgeting spreadsheet will help you to see your money worries in a more visual way, which may help you get back on top of them.

If you're swamped by work or home demands and can't think straight, there's nothing wrong with a list. Several lists if you like. Again, you're liberating your mind by taking thoughts out of it and putting them somewhere else so your brain can safely jettison them. All you need is fewer thoughts swirling and roiling and this has got them out of the way.

> YOU'RE LIBERATING YOUR MIND BY TAKING THOUGHTS OUT OF IT

# Cut yourself some slack

Let's try a couple of quiz questions:

1. You have invited several people for a meal. You put lots
   of effort into cooking a complicated dish. Unfortunately it
   spends too long in the oven. It's fine, but not as good as you'd
   planned. Do you think:

   a) Who cares? It's the people that matter and they've all had a
      good time.

   b) I should have set a timer. I must practise cooking it before
      I serve it up again.

   c) I'm useless at cooking. I don't know why I bothered.

2. You apply for a new job and you don't get it. Do you think:

   a) That's a shame, but I'll find something else. I'll get some
      feedback and incorporate it into my next application.

   b) It's my own fault, I messed up the interview. I'll research
      the company better next time.

   c) I'm just not good enough to do the job.

I imagine you can see where I'm going here. If you answered (a),
you're pretty resilient and recognise that life doesn't go perfectly
every time and that doesn't have to be your fault. You're not giving
up or being lazy, you're just being realistic.

The (b) answers are a bit less forgiving but, crucially, you're only
criticising yourself for this specific thing. You're setting yourself
an achievable target for next time.

If you answered (c), you have taken one setback and seen it as a
damning indictment of your whole self as a cook, an employee
or whatever. You have used it to reinforce your feelings of inad-
equacy and failure. For goodness sake, you just left the food in

the oven for a few minutes too long. And you have no idea how well-qualified the competition was for the job.

Resilient people know how to be kind to themselves. This isn't about letting yourself off the hook, it's just an understanding that self-criticism isn't helpful. Recognising where you went wrong – if you even did – is simply a practical pointer for next time. Not a reason to beat yourself up. Those (b) answers have a hint of unhelpful self-blame to them ('should have', 'my fault'), but at least it only relates to the mistake in question, and we all do it occasionally.

If you're prone to the (c) way of thinking, you could aim for (b) thoughts before you move on to mostly (a)s.* Listen, sometimes – often – 'good enough' is just fine. We can't all be brilliant at everything and we don't have to try. Think how bad it would make everyone else feel.

You can see how if every tiny setback knocks your whole perception of yourself, it's going to be harder to recover than if each individual setback is self-contained and doesn't spread ripples throughout your whole sense of self. So when something doesn't go the way you want it to, forgive yourself, and recognise that it doesn't have anything to say about who you are.

> # SOMETIMES – OFTEN –
> # 'GOOD ENOUGH' IS JUST
> # FINE

---

* Just don't beat yourself up if you catch yourself having (c) thoughts.

# HEALTHY
# THINKING

Our thoughts and our feelings are intrinsically linked. If you want to feel good, happy, relaxed, capable, you have to adopt the right patterns of thought to achieve it. This is the basis on which most mental health treatment is based. Yes, there can be medication and other means of support, but most of the help out there is about learning to think in ways that will lead you to feel better.

Some people's lives make this a particularly tough process. But all of us will feel better if we think in helpful ways. A lot of this is about habits of thinking and learning the thought patterns that will ensure that day-to-day life is good.

The last section focused on the ways of thinking that are essential in building resilience, so that when an emotional trauma comes along and derails us, we can recover faster. This section is about looking after yourself mentally between those big life events, although of course following these Rules will lead to a healthy attitude that can only help at those times. But you want to feel as good as you can all the time, and the people you know who always seem chilled and easy going and happy are people who follow these Rules. Sure, some of us are naturally healthy to begin with and others have to work a bit harder, but these Rules make strong mental health and a positive outlook an option for all of us.

# Think yourself happy

We all know people whose default setting is cheerful. It's not that their lives are any better on paper than anyone else's. It's all about their attitude. Indeed if you go to some of the poorest or most war-ravaged places in the world, you'll still be able to find people who are positive despite everything. If they can do it, why can't we?

The answer to this is that being positive is not about our circumstances, it's about the way we think. Of course, the most positive people have moments when they don't feel very cheerful, but they still cope better than they would without their positive attitude. I've seen several elderly people lose their husbands or wives after decades of marriage, which is always horribly sad to see, and almost as traumatic for them as anything they could imagine. You would understand if they fell into a deep depression from which they never emerged. Indeed some of them quite understandably do this.

It's edifying to see how the rest of them avoid spending the rest of their lives in misery. And the answer lies in the way they choose to think. They have their miserable, weepy moments, of course they do – lots of them in the early days. But then they tell themselves how lucky they are. They remind themselves how long they had with their partner, the wonderful children they produced together, the great times they had. And it's that mindset that enables them to face life alone.

What you think affects how you feel. It might not seem like it at first, but these positive thoughts are a kind of affirmation and over time your feelings will adapt to them. Keep looking for the positive, always see the glass as half full, find the silver lining and focus on that. No one is pretending the glass doesn't have an empty half, we know it's there, but you don't have to dwell on it.

That means no self-pity. Yep, self-pity is all about the empty half of the glass and, if you keep thinking about that of course you'll feel bad. I know it's tempting to dwell on the negative, whether you've lost your lifetime partner or just feel a bit under the weather. But as soon as you give in to it, you've allowed the half-empty glass to dominate and you'll have to work even harder to refocus on the positive.

People who don't do self-pity are happier than people who do. It's as simple as that. Which camp do you want to be in?

I'm not suggesting you should never allow yourself to be upset about anything. Wouldn't that be lovely? But it's unrealistic. The idea is not to go into denial about what you're going through and refuse to acknowledge your negative feelings. That wouldn't be healthy. You need to acknowledge them, give yourself permission to feel upset or angry or miserable, and then consider the reasons to be positive: 'It's frustrating to be short of money, but at least I have enough for the rent.' Not easy when life is tough, but this is about what works, not what's fair or easy.

> PEOPLE WHO DON'T DO
> SELF-PITY ARE HAPPIER THAN
> PEOPLE WHO DO

# RULE 19

# Focus on other people

In a way this Rule follows on from the last, because one of the best ways to avoid self-pity is not to think about your own problems too much. Don't sit at home moping, get out there and think about other people's problems instead.

We all have friends and acquaintances who are going through hard times. Think about how you can help, what support they might need. It might be practical or just be a listening ear. You could drive them to their hospital appointment, do their shopping for them, help them with their CV, look after their kids for a day, help get their report written on time. Or they might just appreciate a phone call every week or an evening out so they can talk through their problems.

This is a great distraction for you and a big support to them, and it's so much more than that too. When you help other people, it puts your own troubles in perspective and it makes you feel good about yourself. That builds your self-esteem because you feel worthwhile (rightly) and over time that helps you to feel more positive and better able to cope with your own hardships.

You're not limited to looking around your own group of friends to find someone who needs a bit of bolstering. Lots of people volunteer with charities or other groups in order to focus on other people and be genuinely useful while making themselves feel good at the same time. Almost all of us have some time to do this if we want to. You might have to give up regular visits to the gym, or the odd night out with your friends, or the odd night in with the TV. We can all tell ourselves we have no spare time, but that's usually because we've chosen to fill it up. You can choose how you fill your time and you can give up one thing to make room for another. You have to decide which makes you happier in the long term.

If you decide to do this (and I really recommend it) you can give up anything from an hour a week to as much time as you like. You can pick a role with little responsibility or one with a great deal. You might spend an hour one evening a week helping at a local sports club or put in several days a year as a school governor. You could organise a jumble sale or just help run one of the stalls. You could even find a role where you only help at certain times of year – volunteering at the local half marathon or an old persons' home Christmas party. The more people-focused the better. It's fine to spend time at home stuffing envelopes for a good cause, but to get the full benefit of volunteering you also need to interact with the people you're supporting.

Remember, this will help you as much as it helps them – it's a win/win. It takes you out of yourself and gives you a huge positive boost that you can then carry over into the rest of your life.

There. See? You haven't thought about your own problems for nearly two pages.

> # IT MAKES YOU FEEL GOOD
> # ABOUT YOURSELF

# RULE 20

# Be in the present

Where do you tend to live – past, present or future? Most of us have a tendency towards one or the other, and they all have their pros and cons. Even if you are inclined to live in the present, however, you tend to do it unconsciously most of the time.

There's a good deal of research to show that if you practise what is known as 'mindfulness' it can reduce anxiety, stress and depression. In part this is because you are more likely to become aware of these feelings sooner so you can address them before they become entrenched. Mindfulness in its basic form is an exercise you set aside some time each day to do. However the greatest benefit is that – like other thinking styles – the more you do it, the more of a habit it becomes, until you incorporate it into other parts of your life too, and slip in and out of it whenever it's helpful.

Essentially you need to set aside a few minutes each day. This might always be the same time and place or you might vary it. Whatever works for you. You're aiming to make this a habit though, so bear that in mind. It doesn't have to be quiet or peaceful, so long as you don't have to interact with your surroundings for the duration. So a park bench or the train to work are fine. If sitting still is difficult, you can go for a mindful walk.

Now comes the tricky bit, and it will be tricky at the beginning, but it will become easier and easier the more you do it. Just focus on the present moment and take the role of an observer. Notice what's happening while remaining detached from it. Don't judge. Notice that your left foot is slightly uncomfortable or that there's birdsong nearby. Notice your thoughts without judging them.

Whoops, yes, that was the really tricky bit I mentioned. You're not aiming to empty your mind, as you might if you were meditating, but you don't want to get caught up in thoughts and emotions either. You *will* get caught up, I can tell you now, at least until you've had plenty of practice. That's normal, but whenever you notice you've been distracted by your thoughts, just bring yourself back to observing them without being sucked in.

This very tendency to get carried away by your thoughts demonstrates the point of mindfulness. We spend most of our time in this state, controlled by our thoughts and feelings, and mindfulness is a valuable exercise because it separates out our underlying self from our responses and reactions.

It doesn't matter if you have lots of thoughts or worries while you're being mindful, so long as you observe them. 'Ah, yes, here's some anxiety about tomorrow's presentation.' 'Hmm, this looks like my usual worry about social situations.' Stand back and look at your thoughts – don't get involved, don't try to fix them.

---

**STAND BACK AND LOOK AT YOUR THOUGHTS – DON'T GET INVOLVED**

---

# RULE 21

## Stress is optional

Here's a Rule I learnt from my son when he was sitting his GCSE exams at school aged 16, and for which I am extremely grateful. This particular son is a very laid-back character, not overly inclined towards effort if he can see a less effortful approach. He would describe this as economical. (I have in the past come up with other descriptions.) Either way, the effect of this was that he approached his exams in a calm, relaxed fashion, without anxiety. He told me, 'I just don't understand why everyone else gets stressed about exams. Exams are bad enough already, and getting stressed only makes it worse. So why bother?'

I patiently pointed out to him that not everyone was born as chilled and easy going as him. People aren't *choosing* to get stressed, I explained. It's something that happens to them and they can't avoid it.

But it set me thinking. Maybe he was right. Maybe stress *is* a habit we can unlearn. I looked around all the people I knew who were either highly stressy or notably relaxed, and I wondered if my son might be on to something. Now, I'm one of those people who is intermittently stressed. That is to say I can get stressed fairly easily but once I'm over it my stress rating resets back to zero – until the next time. I'm not in permanent state of underlying stress. I decided to try out the Rule for myself.

So I did. And I've hardly been stressed by anything since – the results have been dramatic. I discovered that whenever something frustrating or upsetting or otherwise stress-inducing happened, my brain just flipped into stress mode without waiting to be asked. Interesting to observe. My thoughts immediately started to revolve around how much worse everything now was, and all the bad ramifications of the thing that had stressed me, and how much time it had wasted, and how difficult it would now be to sort it out.

My brain was *looking* for reasons to feel stressed or to justify it. It would head off down thought streams whose sole purpose was to ramp up the stress ('And another thing . . . '). Suppose I had to phone the electricity people about a miscalculation on my bill – a very minor frustration in the scheme of things. My stress would ramp up thinking, 'It's taken them 10 minutes to answer the phone . . . *and* now they've put me on hold . . . *and* if they don't sort this out the electrics could be cut off . . . *and* I have to go out in 20 minutes and I won't have time to deal with my emails first . . . *and and and . . .* ' Fascinating. Because it's all quite unnecessary. Half of it hasn't even happened and probably won't – I was just constructing worst-case scenarios and then reacting as if they were already true.

So now I just stop the thinking. If I can solve the thing, I do. If I can't, I block all those pointless thoughts. I refuse to think them, and I tell myself that life is bound to have glitches and here's one right now (a bit like mindfulness, eh?). No need to make it worse by getting stressed. I don't do stress any more, I remind myself. My mantra, if I need it, is 'All the people I love best in the world are fine, and that's what matters.' So now stress – as long as all the people I love are OK – is a thing of the past. And if I can do it, so can you.

> # LIFE IS BOUND TO HAVE GLITCHES AND HERE'S ONE RIGHT NOW

# Normality isn't normal

I have a friend who sleeps for only four hours a night. That's all he needs, and he wakes up bright and refreshed. I know someone else who bursts into tears over the slightest thing. And someone who is phobic about hot water bottles. One woman runs three separate businesses, and another counts things obsessively. And I know several people who are deeply uncomfortable unless they're sitting with their back to a wall. All of these people are lovely, cheerful, popular, and as normal as you or me.

It's easy to worry about whether you 'should' or 'shouldn't' be a certain way. Do you work too hard? Wear the wrong clothes? Have the wrong accent? Worry too much? Are you weird because of your quirks and foibles and eccentricities? Listen, these are the things that make people individuals. It's the differences that really make you who you are, not the things you do that are the same as all the rest of us. I hope you *are* a little bit strange, odd, unusual in at least a few ways. Whether it's your interests or your fears or your behaviour or your ambitions.

I work with teenagers at a local school, helping them write their university applications, and I just love how different they all are. They're all the same age, all been to the same school, and yet this one wants to become a photojournalist, this one wants to be a biochemist, that one wants to study philosophy, product design or French literature. Some want careers that will earn them lots of money, others want a job where they can travel, or where they feel they're changing the world. How great that they're all such different people.

And yet somehow, too many of us get sucked into thinking we should be like everyone else. How did that happen? Where do you think the line is between 'good to be different' and 'not good to be different'? Let me tell you, there isn't a line. So long as you treat other people decently, it's all acceptable. Then on a personal level, of course you want to work on any traits that get in the way of you enjoying life. Not because there's anything wrong with them, just because they're not helping you.

There is no such thing as normal, and the world would be a tedious place if there was. So if you catch yourself thinking that you're not like other people, celebrate it. Never tell yourself 'I'm not normal', except by way of congratulating yourself. We're all not normal and that's good news. Anyone who judges you for your differences isn't worth considering. I know that can be tough if it's someone who matters – your family, your boss – but the point is that it's their stuff and they're wrong. People can be whoever they want to be so long as it doesn't hurt anyone else.

So go ahead, change any part of yourself because it doesn't work for you, but don't change a thing to fit some imaginary idea of normal. That's an entirely unnecessary pressure to put on yourself. Of course you're not normal. You're you.

> ## PEOPLE CAN BE WHOEVER THEY WANT TO BE SO LONG AS IT DOESN'T HURT ANYONE ELSE

# RULE 23

# Evaluate your emotions

Thoughts and feelings are not the same thing, and you don't have to be able to rationalise your feelings in order to justify them. It's perfectly fine to feel angry or sad or frustrated or depressed without having to be able to explain why. Feelings are always OK, because they just are. What you do with them might not always be acceptable – the fact you feel frustrated doesn't justify rudeness – but the frustration just is what it is. People who say, 'Don't feel like that, it doesn't make sense' are making no sense themselves. I've heard comments like, 'Calm down, there's no need to be angry . . . ' but anger isn't driven by logical need. It's a thing that just happens sometimes.

Nevertheless, while no one should expect you to justify your feelings, actually it's in your own interests to be able to understand them. It's not compulsory, it's just helpful. If you can think rationally about your feelings while you're feeling them, you're much better placed to find ways to ameliorate the ones you don't enjoy having.

The first step is to work out what you're feeling. By which I mean give it a name. No, not Eric or Bubbles. Think about which word best describes it. Try to be as specific as you can – don't just stick with happy or sad. Are you frustrated, or disappointed? Is it fear, or anxiety? Are you grumpy, or irritated? This not only identifies the feeling, it also gives you that sense of detachment from your feelings that mindfulness can, that enables you to separate your deeper self from the temporary emotions you're experiencing.

Now you understand what you're feeling, can you think through *why* you're feeling it? I mean the real reason, which isn't necessarily obvious. For example you might be annoyed with your friend for turning down your suggestion of an evening out, but it could be the sense of rejection that has really upset you, not simply missing out on a trip to the pub or the movies. Or not – I don't know, but you might if you think it through.

Making sense of your feelings like this can help to calm them. It's not about having any expectation of them – they're feelings and they'll do what they like – but thinking them through at least distracts you and tends to give them some perspective. You're also likely to notice if you're particularly prone to certain emotions. Do you often notice that you're feeling disappointed, for example? Or pessimistic? Or regretful?

Now that's useful information. If you have a tendency to feel disappointed, that suggests to your rational, thinking mind that your expectations tend to be too high. After all, disappointment is about failing to meet your expectations. So now you can actually work on being more realistic in what you expect from people, or from situations, or from whatever it is you've noticed tends to disappoint you.

Another benefit of separating your thoughts from your feelings is that you're more likely to wait until the worst of the feeling is over before you do anything about it. Feelings may not be rational, but actions can be thought through. And your thoughts can take control of whether you fire off an angry email, or shout at your mother down the phone, or spend the evening at home sulking when you could go out and have fun.

## IT'S NOT COMPULSORY, IT'S JUST HELPFUL

# Laugh at yourself

It's interesting how many of the Rules for a healthy mind involve being able to detach, to separate yourself out, to observe your own thoughts and feelings. It's great to stand back and look at yourself from a distance – it puts things in perspective.

Many years ago, I volunteered with a charity which was all about listening to people who were going through hard times. It's hard to describe just how much I learnt about life in general from this, about how people cope with adversity, and about the ways we can help, or inadvertently hinder them.

One of the things I observed was that there was a high correlation between people who coped and those who had a good sense of humour. Those were the people who were able to laugh at themselves and their situation, even in circumstances where finding any humour should have been a real stretch. I came to the conclusion that the reason for this is that, in order to laugh at yourself, you have to step back and observe yourself and – hey, presto! – you have detachment and perspective.

Of course this on its own won't solve all your problems, but you'd be surprised how much it helps. It honestly can go most of the way to solving life's minor glitches – getting soaked because you forgot your umbrella, or realising as you're about to serve up a meal that you forgot to turn the oven on and the food is still raw. And if you're going through real trauma, it can be part of the difference between falling apart or holding it together.

If you can take the stress out of those everyday mishaps and irritations by laughing at yourself or your situation, you can learn to reduce your stress levels significantly. One of my favourite strategies when I'm having one of those days is to write the funny version of the incident in my head, while I'm getting progressively wetter without my umbrella, or sitting in the traffic jam, or storming out of the shop in frustration at how I've been treated.

A friend of my recently recounted a story in which his organisation (as in he's the boss) had cleared out the drains behind the kitchen because they discovered they were clogged up with fat and detritus. It was revolting, and they put it in a wheelbarrow outside the kitchen door while arranging to dispose of it. Ten minutes later, they had an unannounced on-the-spot inspection from the council heath officer. They couldn't risk the inspector finding the wheelbarrow, so my friend had to smuggle it past him and hide it before the chap reached the kitchen. My friend was wearing a brand-new suit, which got covered in fat as he literally wheeled the fatberg past a window while the inspector was inside with his back turned. Now this must have been pretty nerve-racking at the time, but the way my friend related the story made it laugh-out-loud funny, and I could see that he'd dealt with it by seeing the funny side even as it was happening. The result was that a potentially stressful incident had actually been a highly entertaining one for him.

> # IN ORDER TO LAUGH AT YOURSELF, YOU HAVE TO STEP BACK AND OBSERVE YOURSELF

# RULE 25

# Keep learning

Anything that gets clogged up and becomes stagnant is going to be unhealthy, and that applies to your mind as much as it does to anything else. If you want to stay healthy you have to stay active, in mind as well as in body. And that means learning new skills, gaining new knowledge, having new experiences.

If you don't do this, you'll become set in your ways and life will be repetitive, dull, unstimulating. 'As though to breathe were life,' as Tennyson said.* I fully appreciate that some people enjoy the routine of a predictable life and have no wish to travel the globe. That's fine, but there's still plenty of room within that to stretch and exercise your brain.

Humans thrive on challenge – you, me, everyone. We may all enjoy different kinds of challenge and that's fine. You might enjoy running a local club, I might have fun doing a crossword, someone else might be stimulated by learning Spanish or visiting far-flung countries. Find the thing you enjoy and do it. Better still, find several things you enjoy and do all of them.

But don't get stuck in a new rut. Once you start to find the crossword easy, or your Spanish is really good, go and find something different. All these things exercise different parts of your brain, so mix it up a bit. Don't just move from crosswords to sudoku. I mean, that's fine, but also do something else very different. Organise an event, or learn to paint, or start a small home business.

When you find yourself responding to a suggestion with, 'I don't know anything about that' or 'I've never done that before', those are reasons to try it. Too many people see them as excuses to say no, when it should encourage them to say yes. That's exactly what we all need – things we know nothing about and have never done

---

* In his poem *Ulysses*. Please find it and read it. If it doesn't galvanise you into seeking out new experiences, knowledge, skills, nothing will.

before. Otherwise we're forever going over old ground and where's the point in that?

Expanding your knowledge is as important as learning new skills. Pick a subject you're interested in and learn all you can about it. You don't have to become a world authority (unless you want to) but it's really not that hard to reach the point where you know way more than your friends or your average person in the street. I have lots of friends who have areas of knowledge (outside their work) about which they know significantly more than anyone else of my acquaintance: medieval weaponry, typeface design, political history, wild flowers, modern art, twentieth-century computing, eco-friendly building techniques . . .

What are the things people call you up about to say, 'I wanted to pick your brains . . . '? The topics about which if anyone knows, it will be you? That's not the point of learning – you're doing it for your own edification to exercise your mind and keep it healthy – but the answer might give you a clue to how far down this path you are. Loads of people don't ever get those calls or texts. Maybe their specialist subject is so niche no one else ever wants to know about it. Or maybe they have just never taken their knowledge of anything to a higher level.

> # HUMANS THRIVE ON CHALLENGE – YOU, ME, EVERYONE

# No one likes to be incompetent

I don't like to bang on about psychological theory (I'm certainly not knocking it – I just like to stay firmly focused on the practical). There is one piece of theory however that you might find helpful. It relates to how you feel when you're learning a new skill, and says that there are four stages to learning:

1. *Unconscious incompetence*:* that's when you don't even realise that you can't do a thing. For example, before you start learning to drive you have no idea what's involved.

2. *Conscious incompetence*: which is when you are aware that you're not good at it. You start driving and discover you can't steer properly, or you always brake too slowly, or you keep stalling.

3. *Conscious competence*: you can do it and you know you can. Your test isn't far off and you revel in all those new skills, like your ability to do an emergency stop or a three-point turn.

4. *Unconscious competence*: you're so good at it you don't even notice. You've been driving for years and barely have to think about it, it's so instinctive.

This process applies whether you're learning to drive, or cook, or program computers. And it also applies to less tangible skills like learning to laugh at yourself, or being self-aware, or more organised.

The reason I'm expounding this bit of theory, despite the long abstract words, is because it's helpful to be able to think through

---

* Yeah, it's all those long words. That's what puts people off theory. Experts need to be as specific as possible, which makes sense, so they use the most accurate words possible to describe things – but most of the rest of us don't care for the long and abstract ones.

your own learning process. And the thing you really need to understand is that one of these four stages isn't very nice. Nope, you won't enjoy stage 2 – conscious incompetence. No one does.

Conscious incompetence (I'm inclined to rename it 'you're-rubbish-and-you-know-it') is the place where your confidence is shot to pieces, you keep focusing on your mistakes, you think everyone else is better than you, and you may doubt that you'll ever be able to learn this thing.

And that's the point at which to remember this Rule. This is normal. It's part of learning. Whether it's a new job, being a parent, practising the Rules, playing the violin, or learning to drive. When you start feeling despondent and incompetent, think to yourself, 'Aha! Rule 26. I'm *supposed* to feel this way. I'm at you're-rubbish-and-you-know-it. That's all right then. I'll just persevere and before too long I'll arrive at you're-good-and-you-know-it, or whatever that other long forgettable term was.' And after that you'll be only a stone's throw from 'you're-so-good-you've-forgotten-how-good-you-are' and things will look rosy again. And you'll have a new skill solidly embedded in your repertoire.

> IT'S HELPFUL TO BE ABLE TO
> THINK THROUGH YOUR OWN
> LEARNING PROCESS

# Practice makes progress

I'm guessing that if you're reading this book, you're one of those people who enjoys learning new skills. That's good news – you'll get far more out of life with that attitude. Mind you, I enjoy learning some things more than others. I learnt a new language a few years ago and I really enjoyed that. I'm far from fluent but I can communicate, which is what I wanted. The lessons were fun and, even though I-was-rubbish-and-I-knew-it to begin with, I could tell I was steadily improving.

I hated learning the violin as a child though. It's a shame, but not only did I not see myself improving (because back in those days I wasn't watching), I also hated how my arm ached for 30 minutes holding the thing in position, and I just longed for every lesson to finish so I could finally drop my arm down to my side and rest it.

The thing about learning is the '-ing' at the end of it. It's an ongoing process, not a magic wand. And your enthusiasm won't last unless you enjoy doing it. It's almost impossible to be sustained solely by the beacon of what you'll finally be able to do at the end of it. Months of miserable, gruelling, time-consuming, horrible training you hate, just so you can run a marathon at the end of it? I don't think so. You have to enjoy going for a run, enjoy the challenge, enjoy setting a new personal best, enjoy feeling fitter, enjoy your training partner's company.

If you enjoy learning for its own sake, it stands to reason that you won't be nearly so bothered about how long it takes to reach you're-good-and-you-know-it, because you're having fun in the meantime. And that positive frame of mind will help you to be realistic about setbacks or sticking points or timeframes and not to feel inadequate when you don't master everything instantly. Forget 'practice makes perfect'. Progress is all you need.

If you choose to learn a thing and then you don't enjoy the process, see if you can find a more fun approach to learning it.

Maybe in a class with other people, or at a different time of day, or with an app, or a change of teacher, or alongside a friend, or on a crash course.

The other thing that makes learning more fun is to think about how you're progressing. However aware you might be that you're-rubbish-and-you-know-it is normal, you still want a sense that you're on your way to the next stage. So monitor your progress within that stage, check back to see how much ground you've already covered, and focus on what you've achieved so far. Some people like to keep a progress diary of some kind, so try that if you think it might work for you. The important thing is to think about your learning and to recognise and correct any tendency to focus on mistakes. They're briefly useful to highlight learning points, and that's it. You gain nothing by dwelling on them. Much better to count your successes, however small.

---

## IT'S AN ONGOING PROCESS, NOT A MAGIC WAND

---

# Turn off the action replays

Don't you hate it when you can't stop going over something in your mind endlessly? A problem you can't solve, or an irrational fear, or a situation you wish you'd handled differently, or something someone has said to you. You keep going back to it again and again, however hard you try to stop, until it feels as though your thoughts are controlling you instead of the other way round.

This obsessing, or overthinking, feels very negative and often leads to stress, anxiety, depression. Indeed it is often associated with these conditions but all of us, regardless of our underlying mood, can fall prey to it from time to time. At its worst it can make you feel physically ill and can leave you exhausted and unable to function effectively.

One of the most frustrating ironies of replaying incidents, worries or problems in our heads is that you focus more and more on the problem. What you should be focused on is the feelings it causes. It's much more productive to address the fact you are prone to anxiety, than to address your fear of flying without dealing with the underlying anxiety. And even if you did successfully sort out your feelings about your upcoming plane journey, you still won't have tackled your broader tendency to feel anxious. It will just find an outlet elsewhere.

So what you want is to stop brooding. Ah, but that brings its own problems. If I say 'whatever you do, don't think about little white polar bears', what's the first image that comes into your head? If you actively try not to think about a thing, that can be counter-productive. It's easier to acknowledge that the thoughts will start running through your head from time to time and then decide what you'll do when it happens. Prepare a positive thought to counter the negative one. When you catch yourself thinking about your fear of flying, visualise yourself happily walking off the plane after it's landed. If you keep returning to the memory of your boss tearing you off a strip, remember a time they praised you for something.

If you're going over a situation or encounter that you're not happy about, think about the emotions it engenders, not the situation itself. Recognise why it's making you unhappy – do you feel ashamed, or unappreciated, or guilty, or disappointed or not listened to? Now think about how to tackle the feeling, because that will enable you to move on from the situation itself, which isn't really the issue – just as with a worry that stems from underlying anxiety rather than an inherently worrying scenario.

Ultimately, distracting yourself is helpful too, if you can use distraction to break your mind of the habit of running on this particular negative thought stream. Ideally, distract yourself with something that engenders positive emotions, whether that's going for a run, phoning a friend, gaming, watching TV or anything else. Mindfulness is also helpful here, not only in diverting your thoughts but also in observing them to give you some detachment.

> ## PREPARE A POSITIVE THOUGHT TO COUNTER THE NEGATIVE ONE

# RULE 29

# Sidestep bad habits

Oh how our minds enjoy repetition! It's so reassuring, doing the same thing over again. It gives your mind a lovely sense of security. That's absolutely fine if the thing you keep repeating is good for you – cleaning your teeth twice a day or exercising regularly. And it's fine if it's neutral and doesn't get in the way of the rest of your life – watching the 10 o'clock news, or having to put your left sock on before the right one. But what about all those habits that don't benefit you and sometimes get in your way – needing to eat at 6 pm sharp, or traipsing back downstairs after bedtime to check you really did lock the front door, even when you know you did?

All of us get into habits we come to regret and some people are prone to the more intrusive ones – like double-checking you locked the front door, or biting your finger nails. Even the most innocent habit, such as washing your car every Sunday, becomes intrusive if you start feeling compelled to do it. If these compulsions become obsessive and dominate your life, you'll need professional help to break free of them. But many of us tend to milder versions of this, behaviours that are at their most insistent when we're feeling anxious or worried.

That's because they calm your mind – those reassuring, regular, secure habits. Just what your brain needs when it's feeling disrupted. But not necessarily what you need. I can always tell when my wife is feeling stressed or anxious because she starts straightening objects on the mantlepiece or the shelves.* Straightening things is less intrusive than some responses – it's worse if you feel you have to check all the doors in the house are properly shut or make sure there's an even number of teabags in the box. And there is no end to the strange little habits your mind will have you running around after if it's feeling anxious and wants you to calm it down.

---

* She spent literally years trying to work out how I knew. I had to tell her in the end.

So how to stop when it's getting in your way? If your habits – rituals even – are worse when you're anxious, clearly reducing the anxiety will reduce the habits. So the first thing is to address your underlying stress and worry, which obviously is a good idea anyway.

Distraction is of course ideal if you can do it. If that's too much to start with, an alternative is to replace one habit with another. Replacing smoking with vaping is a very obvious example of this, but when your brain demands you rearrange the bookshelf yet again, you can try to deflect it into straightening the mantlepiece instead – which is much less disruptive to your life because it's quicker. You might be happy with this new displacement activity for your anxieties or you might decide to reduce the habit again after a while. It becomes a habit in itself to distract yourself with the lesser habit.

The most useful strategy of all however, from now on anyway, is to recognise these habits as soon as they start to form and take avoiding action. The easiest time to break a habit is before it starts. So the very first time you're about to go back downstairs to check you locked the front door, catch yourself about to form a habit and stop it right there. Distract yourself, sing a song, take a bath – whatever is going to work best, now is the moment to do it.

> # THE EASIEST TIME TO BREAK A HABIT IS BEFORE IT STARTS

# RULE 30

# Appreciate semantics

One of my family is such a perfectionist that he finds it really hard to deliver anything on time. He's forever spotting tiny flaws in his work that no one else can see and then having to fix them even though he's up against a deadline – or has already missed it. He likes every piece of work to be absolutely perfect. I can see an inherent flaw in this, which I have had to point out to him: when someone asks for a piece of work, they want it both up to standard *and* on time. So being on time is part of what constitutes being perfect, and the overall package doesn't meet the criteria for perfection if it's late.

Redefining perfection like this makes it easier to deliver work on time. Once you broaden the definition, your perfectionist tendency will drive you to meet your new understanding of 'perfect' and help you overcome your inclination to deliver work late. Reframing and redefining your unhelpful thoughts in this way is key to managing aspects of your behaviour that you want to change.

A friend of mine who was thoroughly unreliable finally realised (years after the rest of us) that being wildly late, or not turning up, or rearranging at the last minute, was not all part of his unpredictable charm. It was just damned annoying for everyone else. So instead of thinking of his behaviour as 'carefree', he told himself it was 'inconsiderate'. This had an immediate impact and he's been as reliable as anyone else ever since.

Semantics – the words you use and the way you define them – are intrinsic to how you think. So if you want to change your attitude, your approach, your behaviour, rethink the words you pick. If you don't like being 'painfully shy' don't call it that. Think of yourself as 'a quiet listener', for example, and you can train yourself to feel much more positive about your social skills. The world needs more listeners.

If your self-esteem is lower than you'd like (which is probably true of most people) think carefully about the language you use when you talk to yourself – and indeed to other people. Your unconscious is listening to you and it will hear the difference between 'I failed' and 'I didn't pass this time'. The same language over and over will have an effect on how you feel. Did the interview 'go badly' or did it 'not go as you'd have liked'? Seemingly small differences, but one is much more negative than the other. Are you bossy or assertive? Useless at something or just not as good as you'd like to be . . . yet? Selfish or looking after yourself?

It can feel a bit pointless catching yourself thinking you're messy and then saying inside your head, 'Whoops, no. Rule 30 says I'm supposed to call it *not very tidy*.' But you'll be surprised at how easily you can make it a habit. And once that happens, your unconscious will really sit up and listen.

---

### YOUR UNCONSCIOUS IS
### LISTENING TO YOU

---

# Keep the bar steady

A teacher once told me that one of the trickiest things to manage with ambitious students is that they work hard towards a goal and, as soon as it's in sight, they formulate a new, tougher goal and aim for that instead. Now that might sound like a good thing because the students get ever higher grades. Indeed if grades were all teachers were interested in, it would be a good thing. However, a good teacher cares about the student's welfare too, and the problem with this approach is that the student never feels good enough because they never attain their goals. By definition, they're always falling short. You can see how this can paradoxically diminish their self-esteem as their achievements increase.

A lot of us did this as students* and continue to do it as adults. Some of us didn't do it at all as students** but still manage to adopt the habit as adults. Whether it's at work or in our personal lives, we keep raising the bar so we can never quite reach it. And then we berate ourselves for not reaching the bar that we deliberately moved because we were about to reach it. How bonkers is that?

If this is you – and I think you know very well if it is – you need to recognise how daft it is and change your thinking because it's not making you happy. And it's not actually making you achieve any more either. Remember Rule 27 and focus on the journey. You'll progress at least as fast as you would if your eyes were on the prize and you'll be less tempted to keep raising the bar.

Think of a flight of stairs. Let's say there are 30 steps. It could be a steep set of stairs heading straight up to the top. But it isn't. This flight has 10 steps and then a small landing. Then another

---

\* I'm using the word 'us' here in its loosest possible sense.
\*\* Ah, that's more like it.

10 steps before the next landing. So every 10 stairs you can pause briefly and get your breath back. OK, fix that image in your mind.

Now, here's the important thing: *don't move the bar.* The bar is set at the first landing and it stays there. When you reach the first landing, congratulate yourself. Well done, you've achieved your aim. You can look back down the steps and see how much ground you've covered. Enjoy the feeling of success for a moment. You deserve to feel good about yourself.

Right, now you've proved you can do that successfully, how about a *completely new* bar? Let's see . . . why not put it at the next landing, 10 steps up? Repeat the process and enjoy the feeling of success in 10 steps' time. And keep repeating it.

This is simply a fresh way of thinking about a task, an ambition, a challenge. It doesn't slow you down, it doesn't make you achieve less in the end, it just changes your attitude to yourself as you go. Breaking the task into sections is a good practical approach, but you need to separate out the bars that go with those sections in order to keep feeling good about yourself as you go.

## THE BAR IS SET AT THE FIRST LANDING AND IT STAYS THERE

# RULE 32

# Look for the spin

It's clearly not intelligent or clear thinking to jump to conclusions. When you're listening to an argument or working out a practical problem, you know you need to guard against it. But socially it's an easy trap to fall into in ways that make you feel unnecessarily bad about yourself.

Every so often, I'll remember that I haven't been in touch with one particular friend or another for what seems like a long time. Whenever this used to happen, I would mentally tick myself off for being a bad friend and think how unappreciated they must be feeling. Not any more though, because I now remind myself that if we haven't spoken for six months, that means they haven't tried to contact me either. I'm not feeling forgotten and unloved (because I'm too busy blaming myself) so why would I assume they are? It takes two to stay in touch and, when you live some way apart and both have busy lives, this is clearly just what happens. No one's fault.

Suppose you see a friend of yours in the street and they don't make eye contact or stop to say hello. First thought? They don't like me, they're avoiding me. I don't know about you, but I'm forever ignoring people because I'm engrossed in a train of thought and I just don't see them. Or sometimes because I don't know them well and I didn't recognise them, even though they recognised me. I know this happens because people tell me later ('I waved to you when our cars passed, but you took no notice'). So why would you assume – when it's the other way around – that it can't possibly be accidental?

When you're tempted to be hard on yourself, or when it appears that someone has been rude or snubbed you, or made some veiled criticism of you, don't make the error of jumping to conclusions. Always think through other possible explanations, other things they may have meant, other reasons for their behaviour. Maybe something they intended to say just came out the wrong way – it's happened to you before, so why couldn't it happen to them?

Unless you have hard evidence that the explanation is down to some fault or failing on your part, why assume it is when you could assume it isn't and feel much happier about it? Social interaction is full of little misunderstandings. Hanlon's razor* states, 'never attribute to malice that which is adequately explained by stupidity'. In this case I'd replace 'stupidity' with 'accident' or 'misunderstanding'. To be honest it's much more likely than whatever you first assumed.

> # WHY ASSUME IT IS WHEN YOU
> # COULD ASSUME IT ISN'T?

---

* Nope, no idea who he was. But apparently a razor is a scientific or philosophical law that helps you deduce stuff. Or a thing you shave with, obviously, but not this time.

# ORGANISED THINKING

When you're under pressure, you don't want to waste thinking time. The more streamlined you are in terms of planning and organising your thoughts, the less you have to dither about and the more time you have to get on and do what needs doing.

Of course, the idea is not to run around randomly doing stuff. Lots of us are inclined to do this, because it makes us feel busy and therefore productive. But busy *isn't* necessarily productive. You can run around randomly until you're exhausted and still not get anywhere.

So you have to invest some time in thinking, to make sure that when you start doing, you do the right things in the right way, and don't waste time on things that don't need to be done, or at least not now.

The people who understand the value of thinking in an organised way are the ones who put in the least effort for the maximum effect. They are the people who run large families, hold down senior posts, and still have time to socialise, volunteer and indulge their hobbies – all with a calm, cheerful demeanour – because they're not wasting any time through unorganised thinking.

If this doesn't describe you, and you wish it did, don't despair. There's no magic spell. You just have to learn a few tricks of the trade. Read on.

# RULE 33

# Believe in being organised

This is probably the hardest Rule in this section. Once you've mastered this one, the rest come pretty easily. There's an argument that some people are naturally organised and some just aren't. There's a modicum of truth in this, but it's really not the point. Some animals are born swimmers – dogs, for example – and some aren't. For example I wasn't, but I still learnt to swim and was pretty good at it (a long time ago). Just because you weren't born organised, that's not an excuse: 'I wish I could be more organised, but it's just not me.' Well, make it you.

People use this as a justification for being unorganised, but it is entirely in their control. You're not a victim, you're quite capable of learning to swim, to recite your times tables, to drive a car, to be a parent, to be organised. No more blaming some accident of birth. Accept that if you're not organised, it's because you can't be bothered to learn. That's it.

And that really is the crux. Those of us who aren't organised aren't bothering, because that's how we see it: a bother, a faff, unnecessary effort. Making notes, keeping diaries, writing lists, developing strategies . . . what a huge waste of time. Why not just get on with the job, hey?

Right. Listen to me. That is the mindset you have to get past if you're ever going to be a clear thinker and an effective doer. Stop making excuses. Look around you. The people who never reply to their emails, and buy their travel tickets at the last minute so they're double the price, and can't return the book you lent them because they've lost it, and keep losing their car keys: they are the ones who can't be bothered to be organised, and are pretending they were born that way and it's not their fault.

The people who stay on top of their lives, however, who can always make time for the unexpected, who get back to you when they say they will: they are the ones with to-do lists and diaries and notes and *only one place they ever put their car keys down*.

They're a pain, the unorganised ones, aren't they? I mean, I've known a handful of people who were *so* organised it made me uncomfortable, but it's nothing to the inconvenience and hassle I've been put to throughout my life by people who couldn't be bothered to think clearly. And I'm ashamed that this described me for many years too. Right up until the point when I realised how thoughtless I was being, and that organised people were more in control of their lives. That's when I realised that I was making excuses and that organised thinking wasn't something that you either were or weren't blessed with. It just flows naturally from organised behaviour. If you act organised, you are organised.

So if you want a clear, uncluttered mind and a life that leaves room for – well, whatever you want it to – the first step is to acknowledge that you're perfectly capable of becoming organised and you'll be happier if you do it. And so will everyone around you.

> ## ORGANISED PEOPLE ARE MORE IN CONTROL OF THEIR LIVES

# Learn to love a list

If you're a keen list-maker, you can skip this Rule. It will all be obvious to you, because it's here for people who don't make lists (yet). So what's wrong with making a list? What stops you? There are two main reasons people give me – either that it's a waste of time because you can work it out as you go along, or that a long list is too daunting.

So let's start with the first of those. It doesn't matter how well you think you can multi-task, it's always more time-efficient to do one thing at a time until it's finished, and then move on to the next. And the best frame of mind for planning and thinking is not the same as the one you need for doing. Indeed different tasks on your list may require their own approach, which is why it makes sense to deal with all your emails at the same time, or to do all the laundry at once.

It's actually quicker to think through all the things you need to do, and write them down, while your mind is in organised thinking mode. You'll remember more of them, and in that frame of mind you'll also be able to organise them into efficient groups as you go. So for example, you'll list all the things you need to do while you're out, rather than getting back and realising that you forgot something. Of course something may come to you later, and you can obviously add it to the list, but there will be far fewer accidental omissions, because you started by focusing on the list itself.

Once your list is written you can switch into doing mode and stop trying to hold in your head the things you need to do, because they're all down on your list. So you can get on with the task with a clearer head, which means you can do it faster and better. The key thing here is that you have actually saved time in the long run by sitting down to write a list before starting. Both because you've streamlined your mental approach and because you've got more of the tasks right first time.

I'm glad we've got that sorted. Now, in terms of a long list being daunting . . . yes it can be, so why have a long list? What you need is several short lists. A long list with subheadings if you like, but feel free to put them on separate bits of paper if that helps. Suppose you're preparing for a big trip abroad. You could have a list of things you need to buy, a list of admin you need to deal with, a list of things to pack, and so on. Lots of manageable lists. And – if you don't enjoy making lists – just remind yourself how much less daunting that is than arriving at the airport to find you left your passport at home (we all know someone who's done it).

A relative of mine always said that a good list should start with the following items:

- something quick
- something you enjoy
- something you've already done.

That way you'll have the first three tasks ticked off in no time and you'll feel you're making real headway.

> # THE BEST FRAME OF MIND FOR PLANNING AND THINKING IS NOT THE SAME AS THE ONE YOU NEED FOR DOING

# Think outside your head

It's very hard to operate effectively and efficiently when your head is cluttered. You're so busy trying to hold onto those important thoughts, there's barely any head room left for thinking through the current task. And you keep catching yourself short, thinking, 'Oh, I must remember to call so-and-so . . . ' or 'Oops, I need to check we have enough of those . . . ' or 'Actually this will need to be done before Thursday . . . ' All those thoughts jostling for space make it much harder to focus on the task in hand. Either you forget things or you keep jumping from one thing to the next without finishing anything properly. Or both.

If you're running a big project at work, or organising a local event, or launching into a house move, you'll probably make yourself some notes. But it's not enough to write down some of the things you need to do – you need to write them all down. Yep, everything. Every last tiny thing.

I used to do a job that was essentially project management, and I never went anywhere without a spiral-bound notebook and a pen shoved into the spirally bit. If anyone mentioned a task – however small – I jotted it down. If I suddenly remembered something I had to do, or remind someone else to do, down it went. I kept it by my bed at night so I didn't lie awake worrying I'd forget things come the morning. At the end of each day, I went through my notes and tidied them up. You don't have to have a spiral-bound pad. You can diarise things, email yourself (or other people), cover your desk or fridge in sticky notes, whatever works for you.

The really important thing to grasp here though is not a handy tip about writing things down, useful though that certainly is. What you have on your notepad (or diary, or sticky notes, or shopping list, or the back of your hand) is only one part of it. Yes, it gives you an efficient system for not forgetting things. But the really important stuff is what goes on inside your head: nothing. Space.

Free working memory. Clarity. Lovely, easy, relaxing emptiness. So now you can deal with each task on its own, *without stress*, because you've moved all the other clutter out of your head and onto a piece of paper. If anything else invades your head space, just move it on. Externalise it. De-clutter your brain.

Here's another thing worth writing down – every time someone is supposed to get back to you on something, make a note. Diarise it, or keep it in 'sent items', or have a place for it, so when they don't get back to you, you have a system that means you'll remember to chase them. Imagine how much thinking space that will free up.

I clear my emails every day. That way my inbox contains only items I need to action, and my sent items contain only things I'm waiting on other people to respond to. As soon as they do, the sent item gets archived. Yes, it sounds ridiculously over-organised to some people, but you know what? I don't care what they think. What I care about is that I don't have to remember any of those things because my inbox or my sent items are doing all my remembering for me, and I can keep a clear head.

> ## ALL THOSE THOUGHTS JOSTLING FOR SPACE MAKE IT MUCH HARDER TO FOCUS ON THE TASK IN HAND

# RULE 36

# Don't overload your RAM

Following on from the last Rule, it's hard to exaggerate how much brain space is taken up with everyday planning, logistics, mental to-do lists. As well as those jobs or projects that you're consciously aware need a lot of planning (and that you'll now be writing down in detail after reading the last Rule*), there's the rest of life in general.

However avid a list-maker you are, there'll always be things you won't write down. For example, you need to think through which order to go around the shops: you want to drop off the dry cleaning first so you don't have to lug it around, and you want to do the food shopping last because there's stuff you need to get back to the freezer quickly. But the post office will close at half past, and it's quite a detour to the pharmacy to collect that prescription . . . You're unlikely to plan that out on paper, but it's still using up your brain.

Maybe you're putting up shelves at the weekend. You'll be thinking about what length screws to buy and where to get them – maybe you could do it when you collect your mum from the station? Although actually, perhaps if you went to a different store you could get the paint and the timber at the same time. But you'd have to do that before your mum turns up . . .

Phoning the bank, inviting people to a party, getting the kids ready for a new school term, changing electricity supplier, planning meals, updating your CV: life is full of things you need to think about. This all appears to sit invisibly alongside the rest of your life, except at times of significant overload, so it's easy to underestimate how exhausting it is. Actually, however, it's a big thing and the more of it there is, the more mentally exhausted you will be. To use a computer-based analogy, this is RAM – working memory – and the more information it has to hold, the less efficiently it will work.

---

* Won't you? 'Course you will.

Most of us are used to juggling these things around in our heads most of the time, but when we get overloaded they can cause enormous stress. You need to understand this, because then you'll be able to work around it better. Clear those little tasks out of the way if you've got a busy time coming up – or save them for later – and cut yourself some slack. Recognise that if you're getting to the culmination of a big project at work, it's not reasonable to expect yourself to stay on top of myriad minor things at home too. Give yourself some empty-head time to help you cope (go to the movies, meditate, play computer games, have a cup of tea in the sunshine, play with the dog).

And always remember that this applies to other people too, especially your family. Don't expect your kids to tidy their room at exam time* – if they take a break, it needs to be a proper break. This Rule, by the way, also explains why many traditional fathers don't understand why mothers are so knackered; it's not so much the physical effort of looking after the kids, it's the mental exhaustion of keeping on top of everyone else's diaries and logistical requirements as well as their own.

> ## THIS ALL APPEARS TO SIT INVISIBLY ALONGSIDE THE REST OF YOUR LIFE, EXCEPT AT TIMES OF SIGNIFICANT OVERLOAD

---

* Or, unfortunately, at any other time in my experience.

# Make deadlines your friend

I love Douglas Adams's comment about the whooshing sound that you get as a deadline flies past. I think we all recognise that. And most of us miss deadlines, at least from time to time, if only because we've been so busy organising our lives around some other, even bigger deadline.

Mind you, if life had no deadlines, I'm not sure I'd ever get anything done. Whether I'm trying to finish writing a book when I promised it to my publisher, or simply trying to get dinner cooked before the family have fallen asleep from hunger and exhaustion, deadlines are not just unavoidable – they also motivate us to get on and do things.

So it helps to recognise that a deadline is not necessarily a bad thing. They may make life stressful, but in many ways they're our friends. They help to focus the mind in a way that otherwise can be far more difficult. And it's amazing how often I meet my deadlines simply because they're there.

I have one friend who hates personal deadlines such as, for example, leaving to go on holiday, because she can never get to the end of her to-do list. This is because – and she knows this – as soon as she starts to clear it, she finds herself adding things to it (a classic breach of Rule 31). For example Plan A is to buy sunscreen at the airport, but as soon as she starts getting on top of everything, she tells herself how much better it would be to buy it before she goes . . . and there's an extra trip to the shops right there. Or she adds irrelevant stuff – like buying a present for her aunt before she goes, because her aunt's birthday is only a week after the end of the holiday, so it will save a bit of a rush purchase when she gets back. In this way she has an ever-replenishing to-do list, that she finds herself fretting she can't clear completely.

The trick to taking deadlines in your stride is to be able to cross extraneous things off your list as the deadline approaches. My friend needs to learn to put a black line (metaphorical or literal) under her list and cross off what's above the line. If she wants to add bonus items underneath the line that's her business, but she should congratulate herself for completing the real list and recognise the other items as optional extras.

Most of us actually make the same mistake, albeit in a less obvious way. That is to say that when an important deadline is coming up, we try to fit normal life around it. It might be admin or phone calls that could wait until next week, frenetically squeezing in an evening out with friends, or trying to shop and cook when you could actually live on sandwiches just for a few days. We don't cut ourselves enough slack. We don't acknowledge that we *need* to cut ourselves more slack.

Of course you have to start planning and preparing in good time and all that – easier for some of us than others – but you also have to *expect* the rest of your life to take a back seat around key deadlines. Stop saying yes to things and then stressfully cancel at the last minute. Learn to clear a week or two in your diary and lower your expectations of yourself beyond the deadline in question.

> ## CLEAR A WEEK OR TWO IN YOUR DIARY AND LOWER YOUR EXPECTATIONS OF YOURSELF

# Don't indulge decision making*

Sometimes, organising gets seriously heavy-duty. Perhaps you've got a big house move to orchestrate, or there's a huge product launch at work, or you're planning a wedding. There will be literally countless decisions you have to make. There's the big stuff: should we hire in a removal company or do it ourselves, what date should we hold the launch, how many guests should we invite? And it goes right through to the small stuff: do we need to keep this chipped mug, what's the best font for the name badges, would Aunt Eliza like to be seated next to Louise?

You can spend ages agonising over every one of them, researching them, discussing them, listing their pros and cons, considering all the options. This takes up time – a commodity that is in short supply when you're this busy – and it can also mess up the whole operation. You can't book the removal firm until you've decided if you want one; you can't write the press release until you've finalised all the relevant details; you can't send out the invitations until you've agreed on the design.

And boy, does it mess with your head. Even with everything we've covered in the last few Rules, these things make you feel your brain is under a constant barrage of things to remember, people to call, tasks to tick off, deadlines to meet, decisions to make. So you need to clear as much space as you can in your head, as we know by now (if we've been reading these Rules in order). And improving your decision making is one of the best ways to do that.

The fewer decisions you have to wrangle with, the clearer your head, the more time you free up and the less you delay the process

---

* Yes this is an organised thinking Rule, not a decision-making one. No clues here about how to actually make the decisions.

waiting for information you haven't yet agreed or established. Decision making is a luxury you can't afford when time and schedules are this tight. So don't do more of it than you absolutely must.

This takes a conscious mind-shift, a recognition that any decision (within reason) is better than one that wastes time and effort you haven't got. Sift out the really important decisions and give them the time they deserve. Hopefully plenty of them will be quick, however if it's important you need to give it due consideration. Of course. I'm not suggesting you toss a coin to decide your wedding venue. But, you know, you can decide a lot of other things on the toss of a coin. Shall we box up all the half-used soap and bath oils and shampoo for the new house, or buy new when we arrive? Does it matter? If you don't know the answer, it's more helpful just to get on with it and not waste time and head space thinking about it.

It matters that the guest name badges at your product launch look right, but once you've narrowed it down to two colours, or three fonts . . . oh, just hurry up and do it – any of those will look fine. There are more important things to move on to.

This has to be a conscious shift because the decisions you're glossing over are ones you would have given more time to in other circumstances, so it seems natural to focus on them now. However – think about it* – they're not the best use of your time right now.

> # ANY DECISION (WITHIN REASON) IS BETTER THAN ONE THAT WASTES TIME AND EFFORT YOU HAVEN'T GOT

---

\* But not for too long, obviously.

# Get creatively organised

Lists, calendars, notes, online diaries, pop-up reminders – people use lots of standard methods to organise themselves. All of them work for some of us, or for some of the time. Just don't be fooled into thinking these are your only options. If none of them works for a particular purpose, find another way to organise yourself.

One member of my family has a foolproof and unorthodox technique for reminding himself of those things you only think of just before getting into bed. He turns his toothbrush upside-down. When he gets up in the morning he sees the inverted toothbrush and instantly remembers the thing. Apparently it's never failed. Personally I think I'd just stare at the toothbrush for ages wondering what the hell I was supposed to be remembering, but it works for him.

I have no idea how he stumbled on this strategy, but it's pleasingly creative. And that's the point – you can be as imaginative and as random as you like about how you organise your life. So long as it works for you, go for it. There are no rules.* Don't get trapped in a box where the only options are a to-do list a diary or a reminder pinging up at you.

One child I know has dyspraxia and autism spectrum disorder (ASD). This particular child is bright and at a mainstream school, but struggles with organisational stuff because his brain doesn't coordinate itself in the way most people's do. So the family has become very imaginative about ways to help him remember to do things at school, such as bring home his games kit, or turn up to a lunchtime club, or hand in a piece of work.

This child has learnt to develop his own strategies. Depending on what he's trying to organise he might colour-code things, or tie pieces of ribbon to his school bag, or set a timer on his phone

---

\* Except this one.

(he sometimes needs help remembering to set the reminder). Sometimes he has lists most of us wouldn't need – such as a detailed list of items to take to school each day, where most kids would just work it out from a timetable of that day's lessons. Sometimes he switches between accents to talk about different things, because it helps him differentiate them in his own mind. Of course, people with ASD and dyspraxia are often particularly good at this kind of thinking, but that doesn't mean the rest of us can't use it too.

A lot of people work better in some medium other than writing, in which case other approaches often will win out over to-do lists and calendars and sticky notes. If you're musical, you might be able to harness that to help you remember. Maybe turn your reminder into a song. Using colours in some way works well for some people, or visualisation: if you see yourself baking a cake, going through all the steps, that might be an easier way to remember which ingredients to get when you're at the supermarket than trying to write it down.

So don't be bound by traditional strategies for remembering things, except where you've established that they're the best approach for you. Find the methods that help *you* remember, and who cares whether they work for anyone else?

# YOU CAN BE AS IMAGINATIVE AND AS RANDOM AS YOU LIKE ABOUT HOW YOU ORGANISE YOUR LIFE

# THINKING
# CREATIVELY

This is the fun stuff. You're designing a new product, or organising a party, or decorating a house, reorganising your workload, planning a holiday, or producing a piece of music. You're waiting for your muse to appear . . . However, while you're waiting for inspiration to strike, you could actually think your way there instead. As Thomas Edison said, 'Genius is 1 per cent inspiration and 99 per cent perspiration.' You don't need my help with the inspiration, but I can point you in the right direction for the other 99 per cent.

I've watched some brilliant creative thinkers at work, I've talked to them, I've seen how they operate at first hand. And over the years I've come to understand the unspoken Rules they follow to free up their minds so that the 1 per cent of inspiration can find its way in. Indeed, I've learnt to use the Rules myself. Because while creative thinking comes naturally to a few lucky people, the rest of us aren't excluded. We simply have to train our minds. Once you've established the right thinking habits, you'll find they come naturally to you, too.

Creative thinking is all about seeing where your thoughts take you. You might know where you're starting from, but you have no idea where your destination is. So you need to think in a way that opens you up to possibilities, or plays with ideas, that you might not have considered. If you use your brain in the best way, and open enough doors, you make it so much easier for your muse to get in.

# Train your brain

If you have a current project you want to get creative about – you might even have turned to this page for that reason – I hope you'll find the next few Rules useful. However, what you really want is to become a true creative thinker who comes up with ideas big and small on a daily basis. Whether you're launching a business or just getting experimental with a recipe, you want this stuff to be second nature.

Of course, that means you need to practise. It's no good reading a Rule or two here, coming up with a genius idea, and then not using your creative brain cells again until the next big challenge comes along. That's like teaching your dog to sit and then never asking it to sit until, years later, you need it to sit and wonder why it doesn't remember what you're talking about. Once your dog can sit on command, you ask it to sit once or twice a day, even if you don't need it to. That way, when you suddenly really need it to sit, it's effortless.

Well, your brain isn't that different from your dog's. If you want to be able to think in a particular way, you need to form and strengthen those neural pathways that enable your thoughts to travel where you want them to. That means you need to be thinking creatively every single day.

Trouble is, where do you fit that in to your normal routine? How creative can you be about getting showered and dressed and breakfasted? What scope is there for your imagination in commuting to work, or doing the laundry, or feeding the cat? You might be surprised actually . . .

What matters is not getting stuck in a mental rut. It's those deep ruts that make it so hard for your brain to think in any way other than the norm. Once you train it to think differently over even the small things, it starts to climb out of other ruts too. So shake things up a little. Break your routines. Live a little. Find a new route to take to work, walk the dog in a different park, stand facing the other way in the shower, cook something you've never eaten before, go on holiday somewhere different. And, crucially – make it normal to not have a 'normal'.

Some of these things are small, some less so. And they all add up to training your brain to assume nothing, to look at things differently, to expect the unexpected. Grab every opportunity to get stuck into other creative pursuits, too – write or paint or act or play music or dance. Volunteer to decorate the village hall for your sister's wedding, or design the exhibition stand for your company, or come up with a theme for the Christmas party.

Come on, if you're serious about becoming a true creative thinker, you need to start by thinking creatively of ways to practise. If you don't see an opportunity, make one. Give your brain a chance to show you what it can do. That way, when those big creative projects come along, your brain will be primed and ready to excel.

> # IF YOU DON'T SEE AN OPPORTUNITY, MAKE ONE

# RULE 41

# Feed your mind

Einstein is a bit of a hero of mine, and he reckoned that imagination was more important than knowledge. That's even more true now when almost all knowledge is out there in the ether waiting for you to call it down at the tap of a keyboard. You really don't need to be storing it in your head. But imagination – you can't download that, and imagination is the key to creative thinking. So what you really need to do is expand your imagination any way you can.

Einstein also said the way to have intelligent children was to read them fairy tales. To increase their intelligence further, you should read them more fairy tales. When you hear the words of a story, the plot might be provided for you by the writer, but your imagination supplies the pictures. When you read it to yourself, your imagination supplies the voices and the sounds too.

Do me a favour – go and read the prologue to Shakespeare's *Henry V* if you don't already know it (it's out there in the ether waiting for you). He describes perfectly what the imagination is capable of and how you can use it to imagine even, for example, that the confines of the theatre 'hold the vasty fields of France'. The human imagination is an extraordinary thing, and it's almost a sin not to make our own as strong and agile and vivid as we can.

Reading fiction is essential. And, incidentally, Einstein's point is important if you want your children to develop brilliant creative minds. Read to them as often as you can and give them a love of books. It's no good just watching a movie, where all the imagining is done for you. That's great, but it's an entirely different thing and no substitute for reading. And encourage them to make things up. Small children will believe in magic, and in Santa, and the tooth fairy, for years if you help them. I had friends whose children firmly believed that the family cat could actually fly, and it was a delight to find that their parents had sensibly allowed them to continue in this belief, where many parents would unthinkingly have said, 'Don't be silly. Cats can't fly.'

If I had to put one activity at the top of my list for developing the imagination that you need in order to think creatively, it would be reading. Fortunately, however, I don't have to put one thing at the top, and there are lots of other ways to feed your creative mind. Reading poetry, writing anything, music of whatever kind you enjoy (and remember to shake things up occasionally – don't get stuck in a rut). Plenty of very clever comedians, especially the more surreal ones, force your mind to make unexpected leaps and twists and jumps, and knock your thinking out of its ruts, along with comedy shows from Monty Python onwards.

If you think about it, loads of jokes are based around catching your brain unawares, setting up a pattern and then unexpectedly breaking it. And immersing yourself in this kind of humour, hanging out with friends that make you laugh, watching funny shows, is one of the most enjoyable ways to encourage your mind to think more creatively.

> WHEN YOU HEAR THE WORDS OF A STORY, THE PLOT MIGHT BE PROVIDED FOR YOU BY THE WRITER, BUT YOUR IMAGINATION SUPPLIES THE PICTURES

# Get in the mood

Most of us can't simply switch on our creative brain at the drop of a hat. If you're rushing to an appointment you're late for, and it's pouring with rain but you forgot to bring a coat, and you can't stop worrying because the budgie's not eating properly, this is not the moment you're going to get your best thinking done.

We need to coax and cajole our brains a bit to encourage them to be creative. It's not our normal state of mind – we spend most of our time doing something, not simply thinking. Just consider how often you're focused on a practical task: talking, cooking, messaging, showering, watching TV, digging something out of your wallet, choosing veg in the supermarket. We don't spend a great deal of time just letting our minds drift freely. Sometimes you can think creatively while you're doing something else, but if it's not deliberate your mind is likely to focus back on the everyday. You could daydream in the shower, for example, but it's very easy to find you've actually started wondering if you need to buy more shower gel because it's nearly run out.

So help your brain get in the mood to think creatively. Wine and dine it a bit. This isn't something you have to fit round everything else – it's worth setting aside time for it specially. So start by making sure you can relax. It's not easy to think freely when you're expecting a visitor at any moment, or your next meeting starts in five minutes, or you're bursting for a pee.

You need to know where and how you think best, and create the atmosphere you want. If you don't already know this, experiment to find out what works for you. Some of us think best on a walk, others in a darkened room, or in the shower, or at the gym, or listening to a particular kind of music.

I would add that some of us do our best thinking alongside other people, and that's fine too. There's more on this in the section on 'Thinking together' (see page 134). There will be times it's not feasible though, or no one else is interested, so to be a true Rules thinker you'll want to learn to be creative on your own too. If this is you, talking aloud even when you think alone can sometimes help.

The better you get at creative thinking, the more naturally your brain will cooperate without always having its ideal surroundings. The best creative minds can come up with genius ideas at any time of day or night, even when they're stressed or busy or feeling hungry. That's because creativity is a habit your brain can learn if you practise it enough, as we've established. However, as with everything, you need to start with the basics before you remove the stabilisers.

YOU NEED TO KNOW WHERE
AND HOW YOU THINK
BEST, AND CREATE THE
ATMOSPHERE YOU WANT

# Open up

Let's do some warm-up exercises now shall we? If you were about to launch into some kind of physical exertion you'd do a few stretches first. Well, it's the same with mental exercise. You've got yourself in the mood, now limber up a bit before you focus on your current creative exercise.

There are lots of exercises you could do, and it doesn't really matter which you choose – except you don't want to get stuck in a new rut, so don't always pick the same thing. There are lots of suggestions online and in books, or you could be properly creative and invent your own. What you're after is anything that forces you to think divergently for a couple of minutes to set your mind working in the right way.

Divergent thinking means taking a starting point and heading off in as many unexpected directions as you can – which is what creative thinking is all about. It is the opposite of convergent thinking, where your thoughts bring the necessary strands together into a single answer. Convergent thinking is exactly what you need to solve a maths question, for example, and exactly not what you need to generate ideas.

If you ask a naturally convergent thinker how they would use a brick, they're likely to tell you that they'd use it to build a house. A divergent thinker, however, might tell you that they'd use it to prop a door open, or to weigh down an empty bin so it doesn't blow away, or to smash a window, or stop a car rolling down a hill, or to break into chunks and put in a flowerpot to help the water drain from it, or to stand on to see over a wall that's just too high for them.

Now, while most of us tend to lean towards being either convergent or divergent thinkers, of course we're all capable of either when necessary. Every time you check your change in a shop, you're thinking convergently. When you try to answer the question

'What would you like for your birthday?' you're probably thinking divergently. And when you want to get creative, you definitely need to be in a divergent frame of mind.

The brick question is a really good example of an exercise to open your mind in readiness for thinking imaginatively. Try to think of ten uncommon uses for a common object within two minutes: a tissue, a mug, a phone, a book, a hole punch . . .

If you always start your thinking sessions this way, changing the object each time, you'll just get stuck in a fresh rut. So check out other quick creative exercises and just use this one occasionally. The idea is to stimulate the creative part of your brain and prepare it for the real task, in the same way that a vocal warm-up prepares you to sing or getting your hair wet prepares it for the shampoo.

> IF YOU WERE ABOUT TO LAUNCH INTO SOME KIND OF PHYSICAL EXERTION, YOU'D DO A FEW STRETCHES FIRST

# There are no rules

Fasten your seat belt, we're about to do some serious thinking. On second thoughts . . . don't fasten your seat belt. If you start putting constraints on your thoughts, you can't let them roam freely however and wherever they choose. And that is the key to creative thinking. Even the most unlikely paths, the most unpromising ideas, the most unexpected thoughts can lead to that moment of enlightenment that you're after.

Listen, if you save one part of your brain to run a commentary on your creative thoughts – 'That's a stupid idea', 'That'll never work', 'Yeah, right, how will you get anyone else to agree to that?' – you're doomed. Time enough for all that later, once you've arrived at an idea (or several) worth analysing more carefully, and with your critical thinking skills not your creative brain.

Right now, the object is to generate ideas. All ideas. Any ideas. The time for deciding whether they're good, workable, popular, affordable comes later. Even the worst-looking ideas might be worked into brilliant ones, but not if you rejected them before you started. Linus Pauling said, 'If you want to have good ideas, you must have many ideas.' He was one of only two people to win Nobel prizes in two different fields,* and what's good enough for him is good enough for me. I'm not saying all your ideas will be brilliant, or even that they can all be turned into something brilliant, but if you censor them at this stage you will certainly delete some ideas that you shouldn't.

A friend of mine had the idea that it would be really eco-friendly to persuade people to re-use gift-wrapping paper. Well that sounds like a useless idea because, if it was workable, we'd be doing it already – it would save money and be good for the environment, so why wouldn't we? Because the paper tears easily, crumples,

---

* Marie Curie, before you ask.

and most people tear it to shreds when unwrapping their gifts. Most of us would have discarded this idea as fruitless and moved on. But not my friend. She now has a successful business making re-usable wrapping paper. She turned the idea around from changing people's attitudes, to changing the paper itself. Obvious now you think about it, and impossible if she'd just scrumpled and torn up her first idea like the paper itself.

So at this stage, just try to generate ideas without assessing them. Even more to the point, your brain won't function as well in two modes at once – imaginative *and* analytical – as it will if you leave it alone to do its creative thing unhindered. Otherwise it's like trying to drive in neutral and fifth gear simultaneously You won't manage to do either properly. Or you'll end up in third, which isn't either of what you actually wanted.

If you're hoping to generate lots of ideas, it's a good idea to have a way of noting them down so your free-flowing thoughts aren't impeded by an anxiety that you'll forget them. Once it's on paper, or voice memo, you can think on without the background feeling that you have to hang on to the last idea so you don't lose it.

> # IF YOU START PUTTING CONSTRAINTS ON YOUR THOUGHTS, YOU CAN'T LET THEM ROAM FREELY

# Spot the box

Lots of people will exhort you to 'think outside the box'. There are plenty of strategies for doing so and lots of them are great, productive, really helpful. What most of them fail to do, however, is to identify or describe the 'box' you're supposed to be removing yourself from.

In broad terms of course we know what it is. The box represents rigid thinking along the usual furrows that will lead to the same places those furrows always lead to. But what is it, specifically – in terms of the individual project or creative exercise you're engaged in right now?

The answer to that question is going to be different every time. But do you ask it? That's where the strategies seem to be missing a page, and it's an absolutely crucial question. It's hard to describe how much easier it is to think outside a box when you know where the box actually is. So make that your starting point.

This works really well in business because it gives you a competitive edge. All the local retail bakeries round my way (and yours, I'd guess) are in towns – that's where all the people are, so if you want to open a bakery with maybe a café attached, you open it in the middle of town. But a couple of years back someone here decided to think outside that box: they opened a bakery, with a café, on a small out-of-town trading estate. Not enough units on the estate itself to keep the business going, so you might not have great hopes for the business. However, it's now the best-known bakery in the area and the café is regularly packed. Why? Apart from the great food, parking is way easier on the trading estate than it is in town, so it's a much better place to meet up. Those bakers spotted the 'be in town' box and climbed out of it.

Don't forget that you might be thinking inside several boxes at once (I don't really know what that looks like – I suppose they must be like Russian dolls). Maybe you're trying to design a wedding reception in your village hall. So there's a box you're stuck in that says 'village hall' – maybe you could hold it somewhere else? But hang on, you're also in a box that says 'wedding reception'. Try thinking outside that one too. And of course there's a box marked 'getting married'. Of course you might still end up getting married and having the reception in the village hall. But you could elope, or get married and take everyone for a slap-up meal afterwards, or go to a registry office with two friends, then have a honeymoon (that's a box too, of course), and then throw a big party for everyone when you get back. Or not.

Just because you've got out of the box, it doesn't mean you can't climb back into it again if you choose to. But at least take a peek outside and decide if you really like the box or if you were just thinking inside it because it was there. You see, even if you get back into the box, your horizons will be wider for having spent a bit of time outside it. The box has become transparent now you know what's beyond it. And the chances are that the ideas you generate will be more creative, interesting and exciting than if you'd sat firmly and blindly inside it from the off.

> # IT'S HARD TO DESCRIBE HOW MUCH EASIER IT IS TO THINK OUTSIDE A BOX WHEN YOU KNOW WHERE THE BOX ACTUALLY IS

# Think like someone else

So you're sitting in a candlelit room with gentle music playing, or maybe you've gone out for a run, or to do a bit of gardening – whatever gets you in the right mood for thinking imaginatively. You've worked out where the box is, and you've climbed out of it. You've primed yourself to be non-judgemental and give every idea a chance. So what now?

Where are you going to start? If you empty your mind completely, you're likely to fall asleep or start thinking about irrelevant nothings. You need to kick off your thoughts in some direction and then follow them. And you want them to wander in a direction they don't usually go – obviously, to give them a chance to arrive somewhere new, interesting, original, intriguing.

One of the best ways to get started is to look at your project from someone else's perspective. Almost anyone's really, so long as it has some relevance, because this doesn't have to be more than a starting point. So if you're launching a new service in your business, think about it from the customer's perspective. Will they be interested? Why not? What might interest them? When or where will they be open to the information? Will they trust it? How would they be most likely to pay attention?

If you're planning that wedding in the village hall (if it's still in the village hall – indeed if you're still getting married) imagine it from the guests' perspective – what makes a wedding good or bad from their point of view? The amount of time spent waiting around? The food? Whether they can see and hear proceedings properly? Who else they know? The chance to dress up?

These might seem like straightforward questions, but it's not about coming up with black and white answers. The point is to get a whole new take on things. For example you might decide to focus your wedding reception on getting old friends together with each other. Or on providing a meal to remember. Or arranging things so everyone feels involved . . . each of these would steer you towards a very different occasion, and by following these threads – and it's important to follow them as far as you can – you might end up requesting everyone to provide 30 seconds of film of themselves when they were younger, or involve all the guests in the ceremony itself by getting them to ask in chorus 'Do you take this woman . . . ', or hang all the food on sparkly threads from the ceiling – I don't know. And that's the point: I don't know and nor do you until you try it. It could lead you anywhere but it's bound to be interesting and creative. You might rein the ideas back a bit at a later stage. Or you might not.

I saw a news article recently about an ice cream parlour that wanted to come up with a festive Christmas ice cream flavour. So they asked themselves what everyone likes to eat at Christmas and that led them to 'pigs-in-blankets ice cream'.* Sounds revolting, but they went for it. Surprisingly, the journalists covering the story couldn't find anyone who didn't really like it, and they got national press coverage for it, too.

> # IT COULD LEAD YOU ANYWHERE BUT IT'S BOUND TO BE INTERESTING AND CREATIVE

---

* I don't know if this is a particularly British term for them – pigs-in-blankets are mini sausages wrapped in bacon.

# Make connections

You're aiming to open up new channels in your mind, routes your thoughts have never previously gone down. One way to do that is to give yourself a start point and an end point that you've never travelled between before, so you'll have to take a new road. If you've never been to Timbuktu, you can't get there – even from your own front door – without taking some roads you've never used.

Same thing with your brain. Make it travel a new route. Not only will this help with your current creative challenge, it will also exercise your creative juices more generally, so you win on two counts. Now, as with going from home to Timbuktu, it makes no difference if one of the two ends of the journey is familiar. So make one of the points the project you're thinking about – redecorating your living room, or writing a piece of music, or planning an event, or designing an ad campaign. Now, what are you going to pick for the other point?

Fish. Happiness. Balaclava. Global warming. The philosophy of Karl Marx. Postage stamps. Just open a dictionary at random and pick a word. Yes, really – try to find a connection between your project and *anything*. Just pick something random and let your mind go a-wandering. What do the words 'postage stamp' make you think of? It's very small, it adheres to something, it's often in shades of one colour only, it has scalloped edges, it comes in a perforated sheet . . . Now try to apply some of these to your project. I'm not saying you should redecorate your room in postage stamps – that would take ages. But you could introduce scalloped edges to the curtains or cushions, or stick to shades of one colour, or use decals that adhere to the walls.

Were you going to come up with these ideas going down your habitual routes? See? You might end up developing one of these ideas so much further that only you can still see the connection with a postage stamp. Doesn't matter. The point is you've opened up possibilities your brain wouldn't have arrived at without forcing itself to forge a route between two previously unconnected points.

Of course you won't end up using every idea that is sparked by any aspect of postage stamps – the room would look a mess if you did. In fact, you won't come up with the same tumble of ideas that I would if I tried the same exercise. Or even if you'd tried it yourself yesterday when you were in a different mood. So what? The purpose of the exercise is to force yourself to think creatively and originally and differently. Not only will you end up with a much more original and inspiring living room (or ad campaign/event/ piece of music) but you will also have encouraged your mind to think in a more creative and free-flowing way.

> FISH. HAPPINESS. BALACLAVA.
>
> GLOBAL WARMING. THE
>
> PHILOSOPHY OF KARL MARX.
>
> POSTAGE STAMPS

# Make mistakes

When 3M was trying to develop a new, strong adhesive, someone made a mistake and produced a glue that was less adhesive than usual. When you stuck things together with it, they just peeled apart. So was that a useless, hopeless, idiotic mistake? No, it was the origin of the Post-it® Note.

Alexander Fleming was having trouble cultivating bacteria in a petri dish because a particular mould had a habit of growing alongside the bacteria and destroying them. A frustrating mistake that kept ruining his experiments? Nope – when he decided to study the 'mistake' more closely, the mould turned out to have a use after all. He called it penicillin.

One of the biggest bars to being creative is that we're afraid to make mistakes. Actually there are no rights and wrongs in creative thinking, but we've all been brought up to 'get things right' and not 'make mistakes'. Remember the teacher handing back your work in class and giving you a low mark because of the errors you made? It's ingrained in our culture to see mistakes as a Bad Thing and to strive to avoid them in all fields of life.

This is the enemy of creative thinking. It's the worry that we'll get it wrong, mess up, make a mistake, that keeps us from experimenting and letting go to our creativity. Alexander Fleming wasn't the only scientist cultivating bacteria in the 1920s. Lots of them made the same 'mistake' and did what they'd always been told to do with mistakes – throw them away, cover them up, get rid of them and start again. I can't tell you those scientists' names though, because none of them discovered penicillin.

When an inventor develops a new product, they go through countless development stages and prototypes. Sometimes, there may be tens or even hundreds of versions of a product before the one that finally goes to market. So why don't they just start selling the very first prototype they make? It's because it doesn't work properly. In fact it may not work at all. But does that make it a mistake? Of course not – it's just a necessary step on the way to creating a successful product. If those inventors believed that their early mistakes represented some kind of failure, and they should abandon the product as a result, we'd have no cars, mobile phones, sewing machines, lawn mowers, photocopiers.

A mistake is telling you something, sure, and it's a good idea to listen to it. But it's not telling you that you're a failure. It's telling you that that you've identified a barrier to success, and all you need to do is overcome or circumvent each barrier and you'll succeed.

What's more, every barrier forces you to think creatively to find a solution, which means you'll have poured more originality and imagination into the project than you would have done without any 'mistakes', and that can only be a good thing. We'll come onto problem solving in more detail later. For now, the message is to embrace mistakes and not to shy away from the risk of them.

> # THERE ARE NO RIGHTS AND WRONGS IN CREATIVE THINKING

# Forget about other people

I've observed over the years that the most creative thinkers I know tend to have a non-conformist streak. It's not an absolutely hard-and-fast rule – there are a few exceptions on both sides – but it does make sense to me. The human race needs innovators to drive progress, from discovering how to harness fire or make a spear right through to the inventions of the modern world. However, too many innovators would be unworkable because they'd all be arguing for their own ideas instead of taking up each other's. The world also needs people – a majority of people – who are happy to adopt these ideas collectively and make them work. These people may not go out on a limb creatively, but they are the backbone of a society, the ones who actually implement the changes and establish progress.

This majority of people mostly derive satisfaction from fitting in, belonging, conforming. That's why they can respond collectively to adopt new ideas, to use them in the same way as each other, and to work as a team to implement them effectively.

However, if you're a natural innovator (or a self-created one) you can't always be worrying about what other people think. Most people resist change, so if you listen to them you'll be dissuaded from your exciting, creative new ideas. In Dr Meredith Belbin's studies of team roles, the creative ideas person is termed the Plant. Belbin recognises that these people often struggle to fit into a hierarchy, or to cope with rigid systems or bureaucracy. They can be independent, maverick, even disruptive. So in simplified terms, an effective society that is able to progress needs a majority of conformers and a small minority of non-conforming ideas people.

Just because someone doesn't have a conformist nature doesn't mean they never conform. Almost no one *never* conforms. If you get dressed in the morning, clean your teeth, drive on the correct side of the road, you're conforming. However these people don't conform simply for the sake of it, because they don't get as much of a kick out of belonging and fitting in as most other people do.

This is important in terms of their ability to generate ideas, because they need to be free of the constraints it would place on their creativity. If you didn't want to voice any ideas that didn't fit in with the norm, that you thought others might disagree with or be unhappy about, your ability to innovate would be severely hampered.

So if you're serious about developing your creative thinking skills, you need to be prepared for this. If you're naturally quite conformist and enjoy that feeling of going along with everyone else, you'll need to develop a bit of a thick skin. You don't have to hurt other people's feelings, or act without kindness, but ideas lead to innovation, and innovation leads to change. And, while most people will accept a change for the better in the long term, often they will resist it in the short term. You can't let that put you off.

> ## YOU CAN'T ALWAYS BE WORRYING ABOUT WHAT OTHER PEOPLE THINK

# PROBLEM SOLVING

If you're facing a real problem, you have to think in a creative way to solve it. I've separated this section out from creative thinking, however, because what makes problem solving different is that it's reactive. It's not optional. You have to do it because there's some kind of obstacle looming that you have to get past, over, through, around. And to do that, you have no choice but to get your thinking cap on.

The last section was about having fun with ideas and seeing where they take you. This time, you know exactly where you need to be – the problem is how to get there. You know you need to reduce your costs, or fix your relationship, or deal with an overload of work, or resolve a diary clash that demands you be in two places at once. Whether the problem is big or small, this is not something that can be solved by hard work alone, or diplomacy, or money. This is going to take real thought to find a way through, and doing nothing isn't an option.

So you need a set of Rules to help you think in the right way for this set of circumstances. There's some overlap with creative thinking, of course, but there are also ways of thinking that are focused specifically on solving problems. And those are the ones we'll be looking at in this section.

# Clear your emotions out of the way

Whatever your problem, you need a clear and uncluttered mind in order to address it. We saw in Rule 42 how you have to be in the right mental state in order to think creatively. Well problem solving is a branch of creative thinking, so the same thing applies here. What makes it more difficult is that, if you have a problem, it's more likely that your mind is buzzing with negative emotions, which will only get in the way.

Quite apart from what's going on in the rest of your life, the very problem you're trying to solve may be making you upset, angry, worried, stressed, unhappy. Unfortunately – indeed unfairly – those very feelings will make it harder to come up with a solution. You want to set the creative side of your brain to work without distractions, and negative emotions are a big distraction.

I know that if you're feeling worried, the worst thing anyone can say to you is 'don't worry'. Likewise 'don't be angry' or 'don't be upset' or 'calm down'.* In fairness it's a bit easier to take from yourself than from someone else, but it's just as hard to do. There's no magic wand, but I can give you a few tips.

For a start, it still helps to create the right atmosphere. However pressured you are to come up with a solution, you're more likely to do it if you can remove as much pressure as possible. So go for a run, or sit in a quiet room, or play upbeat music. If these aren't an option, at least turn off your phone alerts, or your email, or shut the door, go and sit in the car – create a bit of space for yourself.

There are things that may clear your mind in the short term. Music perhaps, or a crossword or sudoku, or meditation in one of

---

* I doubt that, in the history of humanity, this phrase has ever calmed anyone down.

its many forms (I include gardening, yoga, painting . . . ). Activities that distract your mind from the emotions that are interfering.

If there's any sensible possibility of buying yourself time, go for it. Time is a big pressure, and will exacerbate anxiety and stress. So even if alleviating the time pressure doesn't make everything all right, it will at least help. Waiting works well for certain problems, and certain emotions. If you're angry, for example, it's likely that you'll be a bit calmer tomorrow or next week. And time can give you perspective too. Sometimes a problem that looks intractable now might seem easier to solve – or just less important – once a measure of time has passed. And sometimes if you wait long enough, a problem may even solve itself. I'm not advocating procrastinating, but if waiting doesn't create worse difficulties, why not?

If you're too emotional to come up with a solution you're really happy with, at least come up with a stopgap, a plan B, if you can. You haven't stopped looking for a better idea, but knowing there's a good enough solution out there reduces the pressure in itself, as well as being an adequate alternative.

And finally, believe there is a solution. You'll feel much happier, calmer, more relaxed if you think help is on its way, just as soon as the solution pops into your brain. And if you think there's a solution, there will be (see Rule 39).

> # YOU WANT TO SET THE CREATIVE SIDE OF YOUR BRAIN TO WORK WITHOUT DISTRACTIONS

# Make sure there's really a problem

Years ago, a friend of mine got into terrible financial problems. It was during a recession and he ended up owing a huge mortgage which was double the actual value of the house, and with credit cards bills, utility bills, and a business that had just gone under.

Every time I saw him he had more stories about bailiffs turning up, or threatening letters from the bank, or final demands on his doormat. And he couldn't work out how to sort it all out. He'd paid off all his small creditors, so now just owed large sums to the bank, building society and big utility companies. I suggested to him (and I certainly wasn't the only one) that he declare himself bankrupt. That way he'd write off all his debts and could start again, albeit with two or three years of financial restrictions – but he couldn't be any more financially restricted than he already was.

He refused. He felt there was a stigma to being bankrupt and was determined to find a solution to his situation. This went on for months, and he grew increasingly depressed and stressed and – thanks to interest – increasingly in debt.

And guess what the eventual outcome was. Yep, you guessed it, in the end he had to declare himself bankrupt. He never really had a solvable problem in the first place – he'd just been trying to avoid the inevitable. Deep down he knew there wasn't a way out of the financial hole he was in, but he wanted to believe there was so he framed it as a problem rather than an unavoidable outcome.

Interestingly, as soon as he gave in and went ahead with the voluntary bankruptcy, he immediately felt lighter. He stopped carrying around the emotional weight of trying to stave off the inevitable, and cheered up at once. The unwinnable battle had been far more draining and demoralising than the actual bankruptcy itself. He'd spent almost a year of his life miserable for no gain, and wished he'd just gone bankrupt as soon as it was clear the battle was unwinnable.

I know I said that if you believe there's a solution, there will be. But you have to be addressing a genuine problem and not just an inevitability. Of course you could argue that there was a solution in my friend's case: go bankrupt. But that was always going to happen, and no amount of creative thinking was going to avoid it – not in any realistic or advisable way (he could perhaps have fled the country in disguise, but that might have been rather drastic). Where there is only one possible outcome, you need to recognise that this isn't a situation that demands problem-solving skills. This is a situation that demands resilience, honesty, self-awareness and quite possibly guts. Don't delude yourself into thinking it's anything else.

---

## THIS IS A SITUATION THAT DEMANDS RESILIENCE, HONESTY, SELF-AWARENESS AND, QUITE POSSIBLY, GUTS

---

# RULE 52

# Check you're solving the right problem

The starting point for a great deal of skilful thinking is to define clearly in your mind what it is you're doing. Messy thinking is the enemy because it's unproductive at best and, at worst, can lead you into more trouble than you started with. This is never more true than when you're thinking your way out of a problem.

You have to know exactly what the problem is and why it needs solving. Look, suppose you're off on holiday, you have all the family's luggage loaded into the car ready for the journey, you've locked the front door, and you're ready to go. Then, to your extreme frustration, the car won't start. How are you going to solve that problem?

Hang on – which problem? I can see two key problems here: the fact the car isn't working, and the fact that you're supposed to be somewhere else. If you think you're solving the first problem, you'll get out your tools and lift the bonnet, or you'll phone the garage. Might work, or it might turn out you need a part that won't arrive before tomorrow at the earliest. So you'll have to start phoning around everyone and anyone else that might be able to fix it, phone your destination and postpone your arrival until tomorrow or the day after, unload the car, go shopping (there's no food in the house because you weren't supposed to be here) . . .

Or you could solve the other problem. The problem that you're here and you're meant to be there. In that case, as soon as you establish the car can't be fixed quickly, you need to focus on another way to get to where your holiday is waiting for you. You can sort the car out when you get home, by which time the part you need should have arrived. Or even leave someone with instructions to fix the car while you're away. Now, can you afford to hire a car? Maybe you can borrow one? Do you even need a car once you've arrived, or could you travel by train or coach? You've got a whole different problem here.

It's up to you which problem you need to solve but, if you don't think it through properly, how can you be sure you're solving the right one? A lot of problems are messy in this way – several frustrations or mini problems become conflated into one big messy problem. And the only way to arrive at a solution that works for you is to be very clear about untangling the knots to see which is the problem that you really need to get to grips with, or at least get to grips with first. Solving that issue often will take care of at least some of the others, or put you in a better position to address them.

One of the easiest ways to lose sight of this is when one of your component problems is urgent. Our instinct, when the car breaks down, is that it must be fixed as soon as possible and everything else must go on hold while we sort it out. However, if you create a situation where you don't need the car for a few days, does it matter if it's not fixed for a few days?

> ## MESSY THINKING IS THE ENEMY

# Loosen up

I remember a group discussion at work where we were supposed to be brainstorming ways to help our staff feel appreciated. The idea with brainstorming, of course, is that all ideas are welcome as a jumping off point and now is not the time to be negative. One member of the group, however, responded to almost every suggestion negatively. His favoured expressions were, 'That wouldn't work' and 'We've always done it this way before'. When I asked him for ideas of his own he didn't have any.

For some reason this sticks in my mind because it was one of the most extreme examples I've seen of this kind of inflexibility. The colleague in question simply couldn't see beyond his current mindset, was unable to imagine solutions he'd never actually experienced. He was as keen as the rest of us to recognise the hard work our people had put in during a tough year – it wasn't that he didn't agree with the aim – but his thinking was so rigid he was unable to let go of his preconceptions about how things should be.

This is just no good if you're serious about being a Rules thinker. You have to let go, loosen up, embrace change and difference and new ideas. Of course not all of them will be workable, but you have to be open to those that will.

I'll promise you one thing. If you only ever do what you've done before, you'll get nowhere. You'll stagnate, shackled to the past, bogged down in routine. At the best of times this might suffice, but it closes off countless possibilities for making things even better. When things are bad, rigid thinking will prevent you finding ways to dig yourself out of the mess. Whether your problems are financial, relationship, lifestyle or work-based, you can't afford to limit yourself like this.

The world changes. The pressures on you, at work or at home, will be different from what they were last year. So not only are the old solutions no longer necessarily the best, they may not be viable at all any more. Fifty years ago, if you needed to get a message to someone urgently, you sent them a telegram. Well, that doesn't work any longer. Fortunately, however, some innovative people who were open to new ideas came along and invented texting.

Yes, I know that's an extreme example to make my point, but we didn't switch from telegrams to texts overnight. Some people held out against technological change for longer than others, wanting to keep doing what they'd always done, and they slowly fell behind. Until, in the end, they had to change their ways. You and I, though, we don't want to be the last to catch up. We want to be ahead of the game, solving problems in the best way possible, not in the least bad way from a limited menu of ways we've managed before. We want to have a full portfolio of options without restricting ourselves needlessly.

So from now on, outlaw phrases such as 'It's how we've always done it', whether out loud or even just in your head, so you can resist the kind of rigid, inflexible thinking that makes it impossible to solve problems effectively.

> WE WANT TO BE AHEAD
> OF THE GAME, SOLVING
> PROBLEMS IN THE BEST WAY
> POSSIBLE

# Don't settle for your first answer

Most problems have more than one solution. If I'm wearing a coat and the weather heats up so I start sweating, I could cut the sleeves off the coat to cool myself down. It's *an* answer, but that doesn't make it the best one. If I thought about it for a bit longer, it might occur to me to remove the coat.

Your money problems, or your work dilemma, or the fact you and your kids keep shouting at each other, or the question of what to do with your mum now she can't really live alone any more, also have more than one solution. And the best one won't necessarily be the one you think of first.

The first answer you come up with is really useful, mind you. I alluded to this earlier – having a plan B is fantastic for taking the pressure off, which frees your mind up to think more creatively. So definitely make a note of any solution you think of, until a better one materialises. Even if that better one still only really warrants becoming the new plan B.

Listen, it can take time to come up with a really good answer to your problem. Don't expect it to be instant or you'll assume the instant answer is the best one. That's a recipe for muddling through life. Every time you hit difficulties, you take an option that's good enough but no more. Is that really how you want to live? Do you think that's the route to success and happiness?

Sure, when the problem is a minor one, it may not matter that much. But remember, we're getting into good thinking habits. If you train your mind to think the best way every time, it will think the best way when it really matters. And the best way to think is the one that leads to the best – not the quickest – outcome.

So how do you know when you've found the real, best solution? There's no simple answer but there are pointers. You're looking for the one that ticks the right boxes – not just the most boxes, but the ones that matter most. So for example, when you're deciding what to do with your elderly mum, her happiness is (I hope) an essential box to tick. Solutions that don't provide for this aren't going to make the grade. You'll need a list (mental or physical) of the essential components of a good solution, and also the preferable ones.

And adopt this principle: whatever solution you come up with, say to yourself, 'That's a good starting point. Now where can I go from here?' In other words see every idea as a beginning and not an end point. Always look for ways to develop your first thought into something even better. Assume it can be improved on. Just don't let this take you down a one-way tunnel. Remember there might be other ideas, other jumping-off points, that would take you in a different direction and that are also worth considering. If there's room for improvement, it can't be the best solution yet.

Sometimes, if you're lucky, you'll just *know* when you find the right solution. Even so, although it might feel like a gut response, your gut will have been informed by the thinking you've done before. That's how it recognises the right answer when it sees it.

> # SEE EVERY IDEA AS A BEGINNING AND NOT AN END POINT

# RULE 55

# If it's plausible, it's worthwhile

If you can solve a nagging problem, it doesn't matter where your ideas come from. So don't limit yourself. Of course you'll do a lot of your own thinking, and you'll quite possibly ask experts, or the same trusted colleagues, family or friends you always ask. Remember though that it's extremely hard to avoid thinking in ruts, and you and I aren't the only ones who fall into this trap. Your best friend, your boss, your partner, your workmate, your mother – they're thinking in their own ruts too.

Suppose, whenever you're troubled by a problem, you always ask your partner's advice. It's true that this will help nudge you out of your personal thinking rut, but it will only nudge you into theirs. So now you've got two ruts to think in. Yes, it's better than one, but the idea is to get away from rutted thinking altogether. To be free, expansive, imaginative, your mind floating whithersoever it wishes. That's hardly what you get when you think in two ruts.

I'm not saying don't talk to your partner. They come with the advantage of knowing you well, and knowing what is likely to work for you, pragmatically or emotionally. But that will also hamper their thinking. They will tend – unconsciously – to edit their questions or advice because they think they know the answers already.

So it's fine to go to the same places you always do to ask for support. But it's essential to go to very different places too, because that's where you're likely to get the most unexpected results, the ones that knock you out of your rut and into new and imaginative ways of thinking.

These suggestions can be easy to dismiss because they're so unlike your normal approach. But listen, that's a *good* thing. Even if they need some developing or tweaking or adapting or editing, they represent a whole new way of looking at your problem. Isn't that just what you wanted? Presumably your way wasn't working brilliantly or you wouldn't have arrived at this point. So when someone offers you an idea that you'd never have thought of, embrace it. That's why you went to them. Don't catch yourself thinking 'That's a stupid idea'. Think, 'Hey, maybe I can work with this. I'm glad I asked.'

Good answers to problems can come from anywhere. I was once stuck on the design for a book jacket so I consulted a five-year-old child (I happened to have one at my heels so I thought I'd make use of it). He had a simple and straightforward approach – childlike you could say – and came up with an inspired idea that cut through all the complexities I'd got myself bogged down in.

Elias Howe invented the sewing machine. He wrestled for years with the design, eventually resolving the key problem as a result of a dream. Not where he was looking for answers, but he recognised it as the solution and grabbed it. The crucial thing is to be open to all ideas, whether you find them online, overhear them in the pub, ask a small child or dream them up in your sleep.

> **WHEN SOMEONE OFFERS YOU AN IDEA THAT YOU'D NEVER HAVE THOUGHT OF, EMBRACE IT**

# RULE 56

# Find a way in

I started writing this book in the middle. The thing is, as you probably know yourself, however familiar you are with your subject it can take time to get into the headspace to write. I could have started at the beginning, but I usually write the introduction last. That way, I know what it is I'm introducing because I've already written it. So yes, in that case, I could have started with Rule 1. But it wasn't grabbing me that day, and I knew the important thing was just to get going, get into it. So I picked a Rule I was in the mood for and began there.

Sometimes, getting into the right headspace is the problem you're trying to solve. Whether you're writing a book, planning an event, looking for a house, designing a product, writing a report, the biggest problem can be knowing where to start.

This often leads to stalemate and procrastination. You're not sure how to start so you don't start at all. After a while you add a second problem to this: time is slipping away. So now you can't get started *and* there's a deadline looming. Extra stress which certainly isn't helping.

I'm not sure I believe in writer's block. I don't think it's an affliction that descends on creative souls and there's nothing they can do but wait for it to pass. I suspect it's the result of poor thinking – it certainly is with me. As a writer, you have the luxury of managing your own time so you can get away with claiming the muse hasn't descended. I don't see many middle managers claiming writer's block when they can't get going on a crucial report. They wouldn't get away with it.

Whether you're a writer, a manager or anyone else, the trick when faced with a major exercise you're struggling to get going with is to think about it differently. You don't have to start a book at the beginning. You can start anywhere you like. The same goes for everything else. Just find *anywhere* you can start, and get the thing kicked off. The problem tends to be worst when you're not feeling confident or knowledgeable about the project. So pick an element you feel is in your comfort zone, or which you have firm opinions about, and begin. Maybe you've never organised a big event before, but at least you know what you think it should *look* like. Great – start there, and let the rest of it fan out from that point. Stuck on a major presentation? Plan your conclusion first if it helps, or think about the visuals you want to use if that's your forte.

It might be that once you get properly stuck into the project, you go back and modify, delete, edit, change, remove the bit you started with. Doesn't matter. It's served its purpose now. It's not wasted work because it did a brilliant job of getting you under way, regardless of whether it's still in place at the final cut.

> ## YOU DON'T HAVE TO START A BOOK AT THE BEGINNING. YOU CAN START ANYWHERE YOU LIKE

# Don't get bogged down

It doesn't matter how free your thinking is, how well you've managed to step clear of the ruts, there will still be times when the solution to your problem just doesn't seem to be forthcoming. You've focused your mind as much as you can, and it doesn't seem to have worked. Well, if that's the case, stop focusing. Put your hands in the air and step away from the problem.

I occasionally like to do a crossword. I'm not very good at them, and one of the reasons is that I'm not naturally a patient person. I'll puzzle away at a clue for a minute or two, and then decide there are better things to be doing so I'll go and do them instead. Sometimes, though, I might go back to the crossword again later in the evening.* And I'm often surprised to look at a clue I was stuck on and have the answer instantly pop into my head. I'm not a brain expert and I can't tell you exactly why this happens, but it does.

Your problem may be far bigger than a crossword clue, but your mind can still do the same thing – whatever that is – and subconsciously work away at the problem while you're not looking. So give it the chance. When you feel you're getting bogged down in the problem, stop thinking about it consciously.

The Rules of thinking aren't only about conscious thought. It's harder to apply Rules to your subconscious, but you can at least recognise that it needs to be given space to do its thing. And knowing when to let it take over is a key part of Rules thinking.

It's not always easy to let go of a problem, to stop worrying over it, to focus on something else. The bigger the problem, the more this applies. It's not so hard to stop thinking about what colour to paint the bathroom, but to clear your mind of fretting over a major relationship issue is a very different matter. Also the

---

* I may not be patient, but I also don't like being beaten.

bathroom's not going anywhere, but any problem with a looming deadline is difficult to ignore.

Sometimes you need to take yourself right out of the environment where the problem is and put yourself somewhere else entirely. Literally. Go away for the weekend or even take a holiday. Spend time away from the people – colleagues, family, friends – who are inclined to rake over the issues. Sometimes their support is great, but they won't help you clear your head.

When you return, I can't promise that your problem will magically solve itself, but you'll be surprised how often, with a fresh mind, you can see your way through it. Or at least identify which paths are actually dead ends and which are worth exploring.

> **SOMETIMES, YOU NEED TO TAKE YOURSELF RIGHT OUT OF THE ENVIRONMENT WHERE THE PROBLEM IS**

# Try a new angle

OK so you've tried focusing, you've tried not focusing, the problem's still there. It happens – if this was easy, it wouldn't be a problem in the first place. So what next?

Well, the sky's the limit. You can try anything next. Just one rule: it has to be something you haven't tried before. By definition, the things you tried before didn't work or you wouldn't still be looking for answers. So move on, pick something different to maximise the chance of arriving somewhere new.

You're aiming to activate your creative mind so you can bring it to bear on this problem. So maybe do something creative. Draw your problem. No, I don't know what it looks like either, but that's not important. Just draw it anyway – it's bound to look different from before and that's what we're after. Plus, it's looking different with your creative head on, so that has to be good. Mind you, if drawing your problems gets to be habit, there's a danger it could become a rut, and we don't like those. So if it doesn't work, how about singing the problem instead? You can compose your own melody or use an existing one, it's up to you.

Of course it's important to keep surprising yourself by forcing your mind to approach things in new ways. So make sure you use a variety of techniques depending on the nature of the problem, your mood, what you tried last time, whether you toss heads or tails.

A friend of mine lives opposite a park and likes to work through tricky problems by walking around the park while talking them out with himself. I've seen him marching round, lost in his thoughts, gesticulating wildly (while his teenage kids cower behind the curtains desperately hoping no one thinks he's with them). Talking a problem through out loud can be very effective – doing it in a public space is optional. Apart from anything else it slows your mind down to talking speed which can be a helpful change.

You can argue with yourself too. Play devil's advocate and try to persuade yourself to adopt different options. It's not that you want to follow those routes necessarily – you might talk yourself round of course – it's that you'll have to reframe your view of the problem and look at it from different angles.

Mind mapping is another approach that helps ring the changes with some problems. It's especially good for the ones where you don't know how or where to start. Mind mapping is brilliant for just starting anywhere at random, and again helps you to focus visually and conceptually on the problem.

> # IT'S IMPORTANT TO KEEP
> # SURPRISING YOURSELF

# Don't panic

There are two problems with panicking. First, it feels horrid. Second, it interferes with your thinking process and makes it much harder to be creative or even rational. By its nature, panic takes over your mind and pushes everything else out, and that's the last thing you need when you're facing a big emotional or financial problem. Once you start panicking you're lost, until you can get things back under control – whether that takes minutes or weeks.

Not that easy though, is it? And it doesn't help that panicking can sometimes seem strangely tempting, in a Fine!-I-don't-care-why-not-just-ruin-my-life-it's-rubbish-anyway kind of a way. There's almost a sense of relief at giving into panic and abdicating any attempt to sort out the problem. However sooner or later that feeling will give way to misery because you've lost more time, you've given in to fruitless behaviour, and the problem is still there. So you need to know how to not panic in the first place.

And that's the first point – it's much easier to not panic than it is to rein yourself back in once you start. The earlier you can identify and tackle an urge to panic, the better. It is possible to stop a full-blown panic in its tracks, but why make life harder for yourself? Nipping it in the bud makes so much more sense, and to do that you need the self-awareness to see it coming.

Right, so now you need to talk firmly to yourself. First, remind yourself that you don't actually want to panic. Next, have a regrouping session. Keep your emotions out of this – don't permit any thoughts of 'this is useless' or 'I'm a failure' or the like to creep in. It's your emotions that are leading you towards panic, so be rational for a bit and don't give them airtime. You're not trying to solve the problem immediately, so you don't need to be in a creative frame of mind for the moment. Just stave off the panic and get back to a place from which you can make progress.

So regroup. Think through – maybe write down – exactly what the problem is. Clarify why it's a problem, so not just that you haven't got enough money, but specifically what problems that causes: the rent is overdue, you can't afford the repairs on the car, you can't pay for your child's new school uniform. Now consider each of these in turn. Often you can reduce a complex problem even if you can't remove it, by picking off elements you can do something about, or where help is available. In any case each issue in isolation will look more manageable than the whole.

Think about how far you've come and any actions, however small, that have helped. Note any partial solutions or plan B solutions that aren't really what you want but are a lot better than nothing.

And remember that these problems do resolve themselves. Countless people can look back and say that five or ten years ago they couldn't see their way through their marriage breakdown their nightmare job or their financial crisis, but they're still here and those things are in the past now. Reassure yourself that even if you can't see a solution right now, there will be one, even if it's a bit messy for a while.

> ## IT'S MUCH EASIER TO NOT PANIC THAN IT IS TO REIN YOURSELF BACK IN ONCE YOU START

# RULE 60

# Get help

Some of us just don't like asking for help. Or rather, most of us don't like asking for help some of the time. Personally, I'm happy to ask for help assembling flat-pack furniture, but I hate asking for help with map-reading. This is because I hate putting together flat-pack furniture and I don't care who knows it, but I like to think I'm a good map reader and I don't want to admit to any weakness at it.

I say weakness – of course it's not really a weakness. That's just my perception.* If I'm as good as I think I am, it must be a very tricky bit of orienteering for me to need help. The truth (my family would tell you) is that I'm not as good as I think. I'm a very good map reader on paper (which is where maps traditionally are) but I have a tendency to think I've memorised the route so I toss the map to one side . . . and then can't find it when the route doesn't look quite as I expected.

This is all about self-image and perception. All of us are happy to ask for help in areas we have no ego about. I'll readily take my car to the garage when it breaks down because I don't see myself as a mechanic and I don't expect anyone else to. However I don't like to let on if I'm struggling with my writing, for example, because I'd hate anyone to think I didn't know what I was doing.**

If you're struggling to solve a problem on your own, it's only logical to ask for advice. So you have to overcome your feeling that you're in some way admitting defeat. That doesn't actually make sense. You wouldn't expect the government to take action without consultation, or a multinational company to launch in a new territory without taking any advice. So why expect yourself to raise a child, for example, without ever asking for anyone else's input?

---

* You see – I know this stuff! And I still won't ask!

** Just a handy example. Of course this never happens.

And yet countless mothers and fathers like to see themselves as good parents, and think that if they ask for advice they're broadcasting to the neighbourhood that they're useless. That's not how the neighbourhood sees it.

Listen, being able to ask for advice is a strength. It's a skill in itself, to recognise when two heads will be better than one. You'll still make the final call when it's your problem that needs solving. And you're not collapsing in a sobbing heap telling everyone you can't cope. You're approaching a fellow expert so you can pool ideas. If you were a car mechanic or a computer engineer and couldn't fix a particular technical problem, wouldn't you go and ask another engineer if they had any thoughts or experience that might help? So what's the difference?

All the skills you ever use – cooking, installing software, raising kids, appointing staff, wrapping gifts, calming down angry customers – fall into one of three categories. One: you're happy to ask for help because you don't see yourself as skilled. Two: you never ever need help ever. Or three: everything else - all the things where you sit between being halfway decent and absolutely outstanding. Be honest with yourself about the areas where asking for advice doesn't feel comfortable and remind yourself that it's a sign of strength, not weakness. If you want to solve this problem, and you can't do it alone, this is a barrier you need to overcome.

> ALL OF US ARE HAPPY TO ASK
> FOR HELP IN AREAS WE HAVE
> NO EGO ABOUT

# THINKING
# TOGETHER

Learning to think well on your own is a challenge. Of course it's achievable, but not without effort. And once you start trying to think along with other people, the challenge gets more interesting still. It's not only your own brain you need to manage, but everyone else's too.

When it doesn't work, thinking with other people is frustrating, irritating, unproductive. We've all been there. However, two or more brains working in harmony can be far greater than the sum of their parts, and it's a joy to be part of a group that thinks well together. Whether it's you and your partner, your team at work, a social group or any other combination of people, several minds can generate ideas and solve problems that none of the individual members could have come up with alone.

I've discovered great ideas alongside other people where we genuinely had no idea who first thought of them because it was as if our minds almost melded together and created the ideas through some kind of fusion. And that's what you're after – ways of thinking that harness together your mind with others to produce results that will surprise and delight all of you. The Rules that follow will show you how to do just that.

# You're better together

My father-in-law was a brilliant ideas person. If I was looking for suggestions for any kind of scheme, work or home, I often used to pick his brains. Once we started talking about things, the ideas would flow from both of us and I always found it hugely productive. At the end of the conversation, I would sometimes say to him, 'If anything else occurs to you later, give me a shout.' To which he would invariably reply, 'It won't.'

I have to say, in all the years I knew him, he was right. He never called me later to say, 'I've had another thought . . . ' He wasn't trying to be difficult, he just knew how his own mind worked. He thought best by sparking ideas off other people, and any idea that hadn't arisen during that process wasn't going to come to him later.

That's not to say that he didn't have original ideas of his own – on the contrary, he never stopped having them. However, not only were those his own ideas and not mine, but he would get to a point where he would want someone else to talk it through with in order to build it up to a workable level. He had several people he used to talk to for just this purpose, and he would pick the most appropriate ones each time.

In my experience, there are very few people who can go from the germ of an idea right through to a working model without any input from others. Almost all of us think much better – at least when it comes to generating ideas – when we work together. Other people can knock your mind out of a rut and set it on a fresh path, while you do the same for them. The right person can help you think in whole new ways you never knew you could.

When I first conceived the idea for *The Rules of Work* (the very first book in this series) I had little more than a title and a vague gist of what it might be about. Instead of developing the idea further in my head, I immediately talked it through with my editors and we built the concept for the book, and indeed the series, together. I honestly don't recall how the conversation went or who suggested which bits, and I'm sure they don't either. I just know that by the time we'd finished we had a fully formed idea that was far better than anything I'd have arrived at on my own. Or, I think they'd agree, anything either of them would have come up with alone.

You should have worked out by now that it matters who you ask. You can talk to more than one person of course, and you can talk to them each separately or all together. You need to learn who to talk to about which kind of ideas or problems, and maybe look for more people to add to your list. Different people can be useful for different projects.

Another thing I've learnt over time is that people like being asked for their input and they enjoy discussing ideas – at least those who are any good at it. I've never had anyone turn me down when I've asked if I could pick their brains because their thoughts would be valuable to me. They're generally flattered (rightly) and enjoy the conversation. So why wouldn't you ask?

> ## OTHER PEOPLE CAN KNOCK YOUR MIND OUT OF A RUT

# Play to everyone's strengths

Have you ever been to an escape room? You know, you pay to get locked in a room with a group of people and have an hour to solve a series of puzzles that will eventually unlock the door. I did one a few years back in Helsinki with four of my family. We had no idea what to expect and consequently we only just completed it, and only with the help of a couple of strategically provided clues from the organisers. Why didn't we do any better? I'll tell you: because we completely failed to think as a proper team.

In our defence, I would reiterate that we had no clue how it was going to work. I must get around to doing another one because if we approached it differently I'm sure we'd do better. In the event, we all just flung ourselves at the task, and tried to solve whichever bit of puzzle we came across next. Here's what we should have done . . .

We should have agreed before we started that any logical/mathematical problem be immediately handed over to my daughter, who should drop anything else she was doing, because that's an area where she excels. My eldest son should have been responsible for any really baffling puzzle where we couldn't work out what was required of us, because he's a lateral thinker. He needs to be left alone to do this, unless he asks for assistance, so that should have been a rule too. My younger son should have been deployed on irritating tasks because he doesn't get stressy, plus he'd be a really good foil to help the other two think. My wife should have been appointed project manager because her mind is naturally organised.* I'm not sure what I should have done. Maybe stayed out of the way. Or just kept everyone cheerful and positive.

---

* And it would have kept her sweet.

The whole escape room exercise is about thinking. That's almost all you have to do – apart from occasionally open a box or such like – and we all have different strengths when it comes to the ways our minds work. This book is all about learning different styles of thinking, being more disciplined or more creative or healthier about the way you think, expanding your range of thinking skills. But however many good thinking habits you learn, you're always going to have relative strengths and weaknesses, and when you think with other people you'll get the best results if you make the most of your strengths.

I'll be honest, we squabbled quite a bit in that escape room. I mean, it was good-natured, but it didn't help when we were counting down the minutes. And a lot of it was because not only were we not exploiting our own strengths, we weren't recognising each other's properly either. It's frustrating when you know you're the best in the room at something but no one else has thought of asking you to do it.

So this Rule is not only about playing to your own strengths, but also about recognising other people's thinking skills and making the most of them. It seems so obvious when it's written down, but once you start thinking about it, it's surprising how often it's overlooked.

> ## YOU'RE ALWAYS GOING TO HAVE RELATIVE STRENGTHS AND WEAKNESSES

# RULE 63

# Think like a hive

This Rule follows on from the last one. I know plenty of people whose mental abilities I am in awe of. People who can think like lightning, or who can solve problems intuitively, or generate ideas like turning on a tap, or get their heads round massively complex logistical concepts, or add up big numbers in their head, or make sideways leaps, or see clearly where the moral compass is pointing.

I have also worked with people who think slowly, are hyper-analytical, or who put facts and data before the human angle. These are all things that I personally can find somewhat frustrating. However it's important to recognise that these ways of thinking have their place, and there are times when they can be more valuable than anything I bring to the table.

When there's a group of you working together – thinking together – try to see yourselves as some kind of hive brain. Each one of you is a single component of a greater entity. Between you, you have all the thinking skills you need.

Even when you're alone, you bring different parts of your own individual mind to bear on whatever you're doing. You're not using the same part of your mind when you're cooking as when you're doing your accounts. You don't fire off neurons in the same bit of your brain to read the newspaper as you do when you're listening to your kids' emotional outbursts. You need all those skills, functions, nerve centres, without needing them all at once.

The same is true of your colleague who is always focused on details, or your friend who endlessly wants to understand how things work when you just want to know what they can do for you. When a big group project comes along and you're busy generating ideas, or organising logistics, or adding up the figures, or whatever it is you enjoy and are good at, the hive is also going to need someone who will reliably keep an eye on the details, or understand how things really work.

So have some patience, tolerance, understanding of those in the group who think in ways that you don't. Appreciation even. Because without them, the hive can't function properly in the face of whatever comes along. All thinking styles have their place, and it's up to the group as a whole to moderate which ones are needed when.

> # BETWEEN YOU, YOU HAVE
> # ALL THE THINKING SKILLS
> # YOU NEED

# Leave your ego behind

An effective team of thinkers should listen to everyone's ideas. However they can't follow through on all of them. Inevitably some ideas fall by the wayside as you start working through them. Others will be developed into something new so you can't recognise the original idea at all, although you needed it to arrive at the destination.

If you're looking for one answer and you have a hundred suggestions, that's great, but in the end 99 of them won't feature heavily in the final result. That's just common sense. However it can feel frustrating if one of those 99 was your suggestion. It's even more frustrating if there were only two viable suggestions and the one that didn't get used was yours.

It's natural to feel frustrated, but it's not helpful. Remember, you're part of the hive and the collective imperative takes priority over your own personal feelings. Yes, even when you feel your idea wasn't listened to fully or given proper consideration. I'm sympathetic, but the group will only be able to exploit its collective thinking skills properly if everyone sets their own ego to one side.

As soon as you start to feel resentful, you risk withdrawing your talents, not getting fully behind the plan, even privately hoping someone else's idea will fail. When you do that, you create a scenario in which the team would actually be better off without you. You go from being an asset to the team to being a downright disadvantage. Your thinking skills might be sorely needed further down the line and you need to be on top form, otherwise why be part of the team?

So the hive misses out if you aren't fully behind the scheme, and you miss out too. Yes you do, because it's a great feeling to be part of a team that is working well together and achieving far more than any of you could do alone. And there are always other opportunities to contribute if you're open and willing.

When you think with other people, you all have to agree on the broad direction of travel and the way you go about things. That enables you to create the synergy that can make collective thinking so powerful. You have to buy into this or there's no point in being there. And that means all of you – not only you – have to set your egos aside. It might help to note how many other ideas and suggestions, from other members of the group, have similarly not been taken up.

Listen, an idea that doesn't get used isn't necessarily a waste of thinking space. It will have fed the creative mood and may, even unconsciously, have been the spark that ignited other ideas. It may also – and I mean this in the nicest possible way – have helped to cement the group's thinking about what *wouldn't* work. That doesn't make it a bad idea, it makes it a useful one. So don't feel grumpy. Just be glad you played your part.

> # YOU HAVE TO BUY INTO THIS OR THERE'S NO POINT IN BEING THERE

# Keep an eye on the quiet ones

Whether you're leading the group – or, indeed, whether anyone is – we've established that you have a vested interest in making it work. Otherwise why be there? Even if it's a work group you've been told you have to be in, it's still going to be more enjoyable if it's successful. So you want to give it the best chance of working.

Some teams are handpicked and everyone is there because they have relevant and useful skills. Other groups come together by chance – an organising committee for a community event, for example, is likely to comprise anyone who was prepared to put the time in, regardless of what skills they offer. Likewise, some people will be there for their thinking skills – idea generation, problem solving, analysis, organisation, figure work – while others will have been included for their practical skills.

Even someone included because they're enthusiastic about making cakes or fixing computers may also be good at thinking. Plenty of people (myself, for example) won't be shy about sticking in their two pennyworth. But not everyone is so confident. And yet, if this group is going to think as effectively as possible, it needs the benefit of everyone's thinking skills, not only those of us who don't wait to be asked.

So always have an eye on those people who don't say much. It's possible they don't have a lot to contribute at this stage, but it's also possible they have just the ideas or solutions the team is looking for and are waiting to feel it's OK to say so. If they're not confident enough to speak, the whole group will miss out. Never assume that people who are silent have nothing to say.

This is especially true when there are two or more vociferous people in the room. If ideas and comments are flying back and forth – even if it's always fun and friendly – it can be quite daunting to people of a shyer persuasion, or those who consider themselves junior or less qualified to speak. And yet sometimes the sharpest observations can come from people who have a fresh eye, unsullied by past experience.

Make it your job to help these people open up. Ask for their view, champion their promising ideas, make room for them to speak and ensure they're listened to. I worked with one person who literally never spoke until the group collectively started to do this – someone set the example and everyone else followed – and he turned out to be immensely valuable to the team and a fund of clever ideas and acute observations. Until we encouraged him to voice his thoughts, we'd been without the benefit of them. What a loss.

> **NEVER ASSUME THAT PEOPLE WHO ARE SILENT HAVE NOTHING TO SAY**

# Question groupthink

I was in a work team once which was great fun because all of us were hugely positive and enthusiastic about what we were doing. We had all become good friends and sparked off each other beautifully when we were thinking together. I have to admit though that not all our fabulous and frequent ideas turned out to be as successful as we'd anticipated. They could sometimes be a bit hit and miss.

After a while we brought someone else into the group. We all liked him and were surprised to find that, although he was a very upbeat person normally, when it came to throwing ideas around he could be quite negative. We'd all get fired up about something and he tended to put a damper on our ideas a bit. It was slightly frustrating to find our customary enthusiasm being subdued.

After a while, however, we started to notice something else. Our hit rate was going up. More of our ideas were achieving the success we'd hoped for. You guessed it – this new guy's negativity was forcing us to think and plan more carefully and realistically, and was helping us to anticipate potential risks and take avoiding action.

A group where everyone agrees all the time isn't necessarily a good thing. Oh it's great fun, and you can all slap each other on the back and congratulate yourselves. Meetings are all enjoyable and, the more similarly you think, the better time you have. Only you're not there to have a good time. You're there to achieve a purpose. If you all think the same way, what's the point of having more than one of you – or maybe two just to spark each other and get the ideas flowing?

If you want to think effectively as a team, you need to avoid the kind of groupthink we were guilty of. Some groups, like ours, fall into this trap naturally because the team members are all quite alike in their thinking. Others do it because the feeling of being in agreement is so appealing that there's an unconscious urge to override other trains of thought. Either way, the quality of your collective thinking suffers.

The most important way to avoid this is to be alert to it. Group-think generally happens without the group noticing they're doing it. Everyone just assumes they must be right because they all agree with each other. No one has noticed that you're holding your meetings in an echo chamber.

Once you realise what is happening, and draw the group's attention to it, the next stage is to address it. The best way to do this is to shake up the group – bring in other people who are reliably independent thinkers and not so likely to fall into the trap, at least not now you're all on the lookout for it. Maybe split the group into subgroups to make it easier to set a new pattern. And make it someone's job (or rotate it) to play devil's advocate regularly to challenge the team's collective ideas and conclusions.

# THE QUALITY OF YOUR COLLECTIVE THINKING SUFFERS

# Conflict is OK

Here's a Rule to pick up where the last one left off. We established that it's not helpful if you all think alike and agree with each other most of the time. So it follows that the most useful group is one that thinks differently and whose members often disagree with each other.

You can see the risk here. If you convene a group of people who keep disagreeing with each other, what's to stop every session descending into acrimony, name-calling, sulking, animosity and – ironically, given the reason for it – dysfunctional lack of progress.

So avoid groups where everyone agrees, and avoid groups where you all disagree. What does that leave? Not so fast . . . I didn't say you mustn't argue with each other. You just have to argue productively. The group has to find a way to express disagreement without it becoming a problem.

The single most important way to achieve this is for everyone in the group to understand that it's their job to say if they disagree, and that it's necessary to ensure the group collectively thinks at its very best. Once you know people are briefed to challenge your thinking, and that you're likewise expected to question theirs, it becomes much easier to take. It de-personalises it.

There have to be rules within the team – often it helps to spell them out from the start and reiterate them from time to time. You might customise the rules but essentially they should include these:

- No personal comments.

- Disagree with the thought, not the person expressing it.

- Don't raise your voice.

- Let everyone's view be heard.

- It's not a competition (for whose idea 'wins').

- Don't become emotionally involved.

This last rule is much easier to follow if the previous ones are respected. Indeed, respect is the key word here – you don't all have to like each other, but you must respect each other.

Positive conflict – and no, that's not a contradiction in terms – is what you need. It makes a strong team even better. Being challenged stretches you. Having your ideas questioned makes you work harder to justify them, or to acknowledge that they have flaws. Remember you're a hive – the whole team succeeds or fails together, because the whole team approves or rejects any idea or course of action. It's not important who first came up with the idea. Oh OK, if it was you, you can permit yourself a little private pat on the back, but only when you're sure no one is looking.

If you're part of a group where, even after setting out the rules, it is impossible for everyone to work effectively together, things have to be shaken up. Either the people within the group have to change, someone has to leave, or the group might as well be disbanded if it can't work productively.

> ## YOU DON'T ALL HAVE TO LIKE EACH OTHER, BUT YOU MUST RESPECT EACH OTHER

# Think up a storm

Brainstorming is a very specific way of thinking as a group. Generally you brainstorm at the beginning of a project or when there's a collective problem that needs solving. It's very much an early part of the ideas process and involves a group of people throwing out as many ideas as possible. The idea is not to arrive at the answer, but to create options for working towards it. So it's just stage one in the project.

In some ways it's seen as the classic style of group thinking. It was first formulated as a technique back in the 1930s by Alex F. Osborn, although one imagines people must have been doing something similar for millennia before he refined the process. Osborn had become frustrated by how few ideas his staff came up with (he was an advertising executive) so he began setting them to think in teams.

However he recognised the inherent problems in simply putting several people in a room and telling them to shout out ideas, so he came up with rules or guidelines to make the process work better. These work because they're based on an empirical understanding of how people think best.

Osborn established that a group will brainstorm most effectively if you set only one problem to address, and make it clear and specific before the session starts. So for example, rather than brainstorm how to sell a new product, it is more effective to brainstorm specifically how to generate sales leads or where to advertise. This means you can focus your thinking on the issue and not get bogged down in what the question means.

The aim of the exercise is to come up with as many ideas as possible to give the maximum range to choose from. We know that more ideas equal more good ideas, so quantity is paramount.

In order to get the maximum number of ideas, one of the principles is that extreme or wild ideas are actively encouraged. This is a group exercise, and even if an idea isn't workable in itself it doesn't matter because it may stimulate another idea that is. So at this stage you're not looking for workable ideas, you're just looking for lots of ideas.

My favourite of Osborn's principles is that no one is allowed to offer criticism, judgement, disagreement or negative comment on any ideas. That comes later (if at all). This is hugely important because without this rule group members are inclined to self-censor to avoid having their ideas judged. If you know you won't be criticised, you'll be much more willing to throw out whatever ideas come into your head.

The overall effect of a brainstorming session is to stimulate everyone's creative thinking process so you generate plenty of ideas in a 'safe' environment and can also build on and spark off each other's suggestions.

Over the decades people have come up with lots of individual strategies and techniques for running brainstorming sessions. Some of them are excellent and you can research and use them if you like. However you don't need to go beyond Osborn's original rules to stimulate creative and productive thinking among a group of people.

## A GROUP WILL BRAINSTORM MOST EFFECTIVELY IF YOU SET ONLY ONE PROBLEM TO ADDRESS

# Have stupid ideas

Never underestimate the creative abilities of the people around you. One of the reasons brainstorming works so well is because one person's daft idea can be the next person's genius solution. If you don't voice the daft idea, they'll never get the chance to convert it into something viable.

My wife and I work as a particularly effective team in this respect. I tend to make somewhat off-the-wall suggestions. Instead of rejecting them out of hand, she reins them back to create something more achievable. My suggestion might be wildly expensive, or time-consuming, or otherwise impractical. She practicalises them.

I'll give you an example. We were lucky enough to have a stream at the bottom of our garden. The only downside was that it had banks that were too high to get decent access into it unless you were aiming for total immersion. This was a bit of a shame as the kids were still small and would enjoy paddling in the water. Instead of just putting up with this and being grateful for what we had, I wanted to improve on it. So I suggested we re-route the stream into a flat area to create a big loop where access would be easier. My wife rightly observed that this would be hugely costly, take considerable effort, and might not work because natural waterways can be unpredictable. However she thought about it, and it led her to a much better solution: why not just dig out a small section of the bank to create a little 'beach'? Perfect. And she'd never have thought of it without me.

I've known a few actors in my time. And directors will tell you that it's much easier to get a well-judged performance by reining in an actor who is going a bit over the top, than by trying to coax more from an actor who isn't giving you enough. Touching your foot on the brake is far simpler than revving up and accelerating. So ideas that seem to be extreme or off-the-wall are often the easiest to turn into good ideas.

You must have – or find – the confidence to make suggestions even when you think other people might judge them negatively. I have a line I like to use in this situation: 'I've got a stupid idea but I'm going to say it because someone might turn it into a good idea.' This works for two reasons. First, you don't have to worry people will judge you for having a stupid idea because you've already made it clear you recognise it as such. And second, instead of rejecting it out of hand (hopefully they wouldn't but who knows), the rest of the group is likely to give reasonable consideration to whether there's the kernel of a good idea they can build on.

Similarly make sure the people around you know that they are always allowed to air 'stupid' ideas without fear of censure, and make sure you listen to see if you can think them into more practical ones.

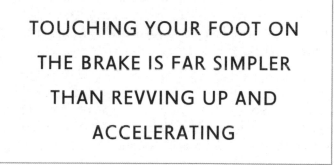

**TOUCHING YOUR FOOT ON THE BRAKE IS FAR SIMPLER THAN REVVING UP AND ACCELERATING**

# Keep in synch

When you're part of a group that thinks together – long term or short term – you are unlikely to spend all of your time together. You might be together from nine to five, but it's unlikely you'll be focused on working as a group for all that time. You might be in the same room but working on separate tasks. Other groups come together for just for an hour a week or a month.

So there will be time apart, and perhaps lots of it. Up to a point this is a good thing. Obviously it helps you avoid getting on each other's wick, plus it gives you all time to assimilate after your group thinking sessions. Sometimes ideas, problems, issues, thoughts will come to you after a group session because you have a bit of space to think alone. This is really useful, and it's common for someone to message the group to say, 'I've been thinking . . .' Your brain may thrive on the excitement of generating ideas together, but it might be more analytical once it has a bit of peace and quiet.

You're still a team though. Whether you're a work department or an organising committee or a family or a project team, the group still exists in non-physical form while you're apart. There will be emails sent, notes made, research done, tasks completed, in between meetings. And this is important, because it confirms and consolidates the group identity.

You'll do your best collective thinking when you're together, but in order to be able to do that you have to walk into the room and pick up where you left off last time you were together, in terms of feeling like a cohesive team and being able to spark off each other when you brainstorm ideas or tackle problems or make decisions or organise tasks. You don't want to have to learn to function as a team from scratch every time you get together.

So look, you have to keep on top of this stuff all the time. You have to make sure the group *feels* like a group whether it's meeting together or not. Good communication is vital. It ensures you're still together and still travelling in the same direction. At the end of each meeting there are likely to be independent tasks allocated – thinking ones or practical ones – and it's important that you keep in touch over them because that keeps you in synch with one another.

It's not just about what people need to know, it's about how they need to feel. Communicating when you're apart reaffirms the group's identity, reminds you all that you belong together, and highlights any possible problems in good time to deal with them before they interfere with the group's ability to work together. Don't just share the information you feel you must with the minimum number of people. Share non-essential communications with everyone from time to time to ensure the team touches base regularly.

> IT'S NOT JUST ABOUT WHAT
> PEOPLE NEED TO KNOW,
> IT'S ABOUT HOW THEY
> NEED TO FEEL

# MAKING
# DECISIONS

In practical terms, the crunch times for your thinking skills come when you have to make decisions. Especially the big decisions: changing jobs, moving house, spending large sums of money, living with someone (your partner, your parents, a friend), starting a business, starting a family. Being able to think clearly enough to get these decisions right is essential. A lot of less significant decisions still affect your quality of life and, anyway, they're good thinking practice for when the big ones come along.

It's obviously going to matter to you that you get these decisions right. And, more than that, it matters that you *know* you're getting them right. Your own confidence in the choices you make is really important – you're unlikely to regret a decision you believe deep down was right, and the upheaval of changing jobs, moving house, getting married, going to uni, getting the builders in, or whatever, is going to be far less stressful if you do it with an underlying self-assurance that it's the right thing.

The fact is that only you can make decisions for yourself. You can solicit any amount of advice from friends or experts, but in the end these big choices will always have an emotional and subjective component which only you understand. So you have to be able to think your way through these things for yourself, if you're going to arrive at a decision that you have real confidence in. The following Rules will enable you to do just that.

# RULE 71

# Decide what you're deciding

Well, duh! No, hang on. Actually it's surprisingly easy to make the wrong decision by mistake. Usually that's because we fall into the trap of focusing on the means rather than the end. I worked with someone who was quite sure she wanted to leave her job and go freelance. We had a long chat about it. She was unhappy and felt that working for herself would be a way of avoiding the problems she encountered as an employee. As we talked, however, it became clear that she hadn't fully considered the implications of being freelance. Once she thought about it, she realised that the insecurity that goes along with freelancing really wouldn't suit her. In the end she decided the best solution to her problems was to change careers and stay in employment. You see, she was focused on the wrong decision – should she go freelance – instead of getting to the root of it and asking herself how to get away from an unrewarding job.

As with problem solving, it's an easy mistake to make and it can lead to some terrible decisions. Imagine if my colleague had gone ahead with her original plan. She could have been anxious and unhappy for a long time before realising that freelancing had been the wrong choice.

So how to avoid making the wrong decision? The easiest way is to emulate a three-year-old child and keep asking 'Why?' until you've got to the bottom of the problem that needs addressing. Whether you're choosing a university, appointing a new member of staff, or building a house extension, keep working back until you get to the crux of it.

OK, suppose you're deciding which uni to apply for. Why do you want to go to uni in the first place? There are more possible reasons than you might initially think. Do you want to learn about something that fascinates you? Or get a degree that will open doors to a particular career? Or spend three years somewhere fun while you grow up a bit and decide what to do next? Or something else? Or a mix of these? You should be able to see that until you understand *why* you want to study, you can't know *where* you want to study, or which course to apply for, or even – possibly – whether you really want to go at all.

Or you might want to start your own business for one of several reasons: you want more flexible hours, or you don't like working for other people, or you think you'll earn more, or you can't find a job, or you have a particular brilliant idea for a product, or you've always wanted to own a bookshop/be a photographer/work in sewage disposal. Again, drill down into these, asking 'why' as you go, until you're confident that you've reached the foundation of the decision.

Not only is this thought process vital in itself, you'll find over the course of the next few Rules that unless you've got this bit of the decision making right, you'll struggle with the later stages.

---

## KEEP ASKING 'WHY?' UNTIL YOU'VE GOT TO THE BOTTOM OF THE PROBLEM

---

# RULE 72

# Don't start at square two

Most of us, a lot of the time, start our decision making at square two. You know you want to change jobs; the question is what kind of new work should you look for. Or you need to move house to somewhere bigger, but where? Or which university course should you apply to?

These all seem like reasonable challenges to set yourself, but you need to go back to square one with all of them. Maybe square one still leads to square two, but think it through consciously to be sure it does. Here is square one for the examples I've just given you:

- Are you sure you want to change jobs? Or could you change whatever you don't like about your current job – ask for a pay rise, or transfer, or go part time, or work from home, or sit at a different desk?

- Need to move house? It might be cheaper to extend your present house if space is the problem. Or rent out rooms if running costs are the issue.

- Heading to uni? Have you consciously ruled out going straight into a job, or taking time out, or doing an apprenticeship of some kind?

Square one means sticking with what you're currently doing, with adjustments. Of course very often square two does turn out to be the next step. Not always though, and the status quo – square one – is almost always the cheapest, simplest, quickest option. Even if it needs a bit of tweaking. This is where clear, logical thinking is so important.

I remember a friend who was setting up a business from home, and was about to build a cabin in the back garden because she needed somewhere to run it from and store her stock. This was going to cost a fair bit, as the cabin would need heating and lighting and so on. She was busy getting quotes from builders and trying to minimise the costs, when she realised that she had a room in the house that almost never got used. With a bit of rejigging she could free it up completely and run the business from there instead. Not only cheaper but also much more convenient. She'd started at square two: 'I need to build a space to run the business from' instead of square one: 'Do I need to build a space to run the business from? Or do I already have one?' It can be hard to look at your living space in a whole new way, but this kind of thinking process can save you huge stress, upheaval and expense.

It's surprising how few people routinely practise this kind of thinking skill. To a Rules thinker, however, this should be instinctive. Any time you are about to embark on a change that will be costly or stressful, always make sure you really need to do it. I'm not arguing against change in itself – it can be fun, exciting and shake us up in a good way. However this is about decisions that are prompted by some kind of dissatisfaction with the way things currently are, or an enforced change such as leaving school, or redundancy. The tendency can be to think you need much bigger changes than maybe you do. Doing nothing – with a few tweaks – should always be one of the options on the table if it's available.

> # THE STATUS QUO IS ALMOST ALWAYS THE CHEAPEST, SIMPLEST, QUICKEST OPTION. EVEN IF IT NEEDS A BIT OF TWEAKING

# Set yourself boundaries

You're moving house. Money is no object and you don't mind where you live, even abroad. You could choose somewhere really large, that maybe needs renovating. Although a little country cottage would be sweet. Or perhaps a city flat or a maisonette. Hey, it could be fun to convert a windmill! Or maybe build your own place from scratch . . .

How wonderful to have so many options. Except, actually, where on earth do you start? You could move *literally* anywhere. It would be much easier to have a few constraints really: being within an hour's commute from work, or near your parents, or within a certain budget, or in a village, or with a garden. Of course most of us have constraints whether we want them or not, but you can see how they actually help.

Up to a point. The danger is in making the parameters too narrow. For example, maybe you need a garden. Not because you're interested in planting and sowing and mowing and barbeques and growing your own vegetables, but because you need a garden for the dog. Perhaps, however, the perfect house for you is out there – it ticks every other box and it's under budget – but you won't look at it because it has no garden. That's a real shame, because that tiny little courtyard at the back has a gate that opens straight on to a big park. Only you'll never know what a wonderful house you missed out on, because you created a constraint you didn't need.*

We're back to focused thinking again, and asking 'why' for each of your constraints. Why a garden? Why at least three bedrooms? Why near a mainline station? Once you've examined each constraint, of course some of them are likely to remain in place, but others may shift. For example, the house doesn't need a garden. It needs 'somewhere for the dog'. That's ideal, because it means

---

* It had such a spacious kitchen, too . . . oh, never mind.

you're opening yourself up to more potential solutions – more houses that could work or, in other decisions, more careers to go into, more ways to sell your products, more venues to hold your wedding at.

The three most common parameters for almost any decision are speed, cost and quality. However, as you can see from the example of moving house, there are countless other boundaries you might want to set. And every one of them will make the process both easier and harder. Each one helps you shortlist, but it also risks eliminating what might have been perfect answers.

This is the time to introduce other options you hadn't considered, like a house with no garden. Do you really need three bedrooms? Or maybe just space for when all your kids visit at once – so probably three bedrooms, but maybe some other configuration. Does the kitchen have to be big enough to seat eight round the table or would a separate dining room do the trick? Or somewhere with scope to knock two rooms together?

Whatever the decision, setting the boundaries not only saves you from muddying the process with options you don't want, but also forces you to think smart and open up possibilities you might not have considered.

> # THE THREE MOST COMMON PARAMETERS FOR ALMOST ANY DECISION ARE SPEED, COST AND QUALITY

# Untangle the knots first

Some decisions are especially complicated because they're interwoven with other decisions. You don't know what to do about A until you've sorted out B, but B is dependent on C. Sometimes they intermesh so that you've no idea where to start, let alone what to decide. One couple I know was trying to decide whether to move to London (150 miles away), where to send their child to school, and she was considering cutting her working hours to free up time to retrain. And if so, what should she retrain as? They couldn't see how to make any of these decisions until after they'd made the others. This kind of knotty problem often leads to stalling and procrastination,* simply because it's so overwhelming.

However, if you muster all your thinking skills you *can* untangle this kind of knotty problem. Trust me. First of all, put any of the elements you can into series. There may be no point thinking about where to send your child to school until you know where you'll be living. If you don't move to London, the options for retraining will be limited by what courses are available locally so, again, the 'London or not' decision needs to come first.

Not only will this clear things a bit, it will also show up whether you need to reprioritise. Perhaps, when you look at it like this, you'll realise that your choice of school is really important to you, and you don't want it to be reliant on where you live – you'd rather fit your location around the school, not the other way around.

Good. You're making headway. Some decisions are on hold until you know where you're living and you've gained a sense of priority about the decisions that will come first. Suppose this train of thought made you realise that the choice of school is the most important thing. That has now become a parameter for your other

---

* Let's deal with procrastination later. It can wait . . .

decisions: must be near a suitable school. Maybe even a specific school – in which case the location issue is solved too.

OK, that all helped, but there are still some interlinked decisions left. So the next thing to do is to think through each one in isolation. Suppose – for the sake of argument – the other complications weren't there. In an ideal world, what discipline would you want to retrain in? It's much easier to think this through when your head isn't cluttered with all the other stuff. It may be that you don't end up with your ideal solution, but I can't emphasise enough the importance of knowing what that ideal answer is. That way you'll make a conscious decision – on the balance of benefits – about how far you're compromising on it.

You should find that by the time you've gone through this sequence – put the decisions you can into series, prioritise those you can't, then think through each in isolation – everything will start to become clear. My friend did this and realised that she'd nearly made a decision she'd have regretted (retraining in a discipline because it was available, not because she really wanted to do it). Separating out the thinking process had given her the clarity she needed.

> IT'S MUCH EASIER TO THINK
> THIS THROUGH WHEN YOUR
> HEAD ISN'T CLUTTERED WITH
> ALL THE OTHER STUFF

# RULE 75

# Go for Goldilocks

Most decisions of any size will need some research – in other words collecting information. Costs, timescales, options, opinions and so on. I say most because there are a few very subjective decisions (do I want kids?) where collecting your thoughts is more use than collecting information. For everything else, you need catalogues, job adverts, prices, prospectuses, lists of contacts, technical information.

And don't forget that a lot of decisions will rely to some degree on other people's feelings. How do the team feel about a new management structure, what do the children think of moving house, will the neighbours object if you put in for an extension, is your business partner OK with you going part time, would your elderly dad be happy to move in with you? This is all relevant information so you need to canvass opinions about any proposed change. This is not the same as asking advice – this is about finding out whether other interested parties are on board with any plans you make. You won't necessarily do what they want, but you need to know how they'll react to your decision.

Frankly, there's a lot to know when it comes to some decisions. And you could spend a long time gathering all the facts and opinions you need. Potentially, you could spend so long researching that you never actually make the decision at all.* I have one friend who explored leaving a job he hated for literally ten years before finally doing something about it.

So you have to find a balance when it comes to research. A Goldilocks level of information – not too much, not too little. Just right. Enough to make a well-informed decision, but not so much you're overwhelmed by it and can't see the wood for the trees. So how much information do you actually need then?

Look, I can't answer that question because it depends on the decision. You need to think through which bits of research are

---

* I haven't forgotten about procrastination. I'll get on to it at some point.

necessary *at this stage* of the decision. Don't clutter your head with anything that you don't need yet. In any case, depending on which way the decision goes, you could just be wasting your time.

Suppose you're considering applying for a particular job. At this point, the only information you need is what feeds in to the decision of whether or not to apply. So probably the job description, the salary, the location, the career prospects (within the company or when you move on again). And an outline sense of whether that employer is seen as a decent one. That's most of what you need to decide if you're going to apply. And if that convinces you *not* to put in an application, any other information gathering will have been a waste of time. So sift out this essential information from all the other stuff which will just get in the way.

Once you actually apply (if you do), that's the point at which you'd start researching for your next decision: will you take the job if it's offered to you (come on, you're a Rules player, 'course they're going to offer it to you). *Now* you probably want to find out more detail about the company, the working hours, the amount of travelling, the people you'd be working with, how the company is viewed within the industry and by staff, and so on. In other words, most of the research you'd need in order to do well at interview, plus some more info on top of that. But don't waste your time on this stuff until you've made the first decision or you'll just be making it harder for yourself.

> # DON'T CLUTTER YOUR HEAD WITH ANYTHING THAT YOU DON'T NEED YET

# Vet your advisors

When a big decision comes along, we generally ask other people for their input – colleagues, family, friends, professionals. People who don't have a vested interest in the outcome, but who we reckon will be able to give us a balanced, unbiased opinion.

Ah, if only. But there's no such thing as an unbiased opinion, by definition. Facts may be unbiased (although which facts? I'll come to that in a minute . . . ) but an opinion is always a personal standpoint, and everyone has their own take.

Suppose you're thinking of investing in the property market and you know someone who has done the same thing themselves. Ideal! They'll be able to give you the lowdown, won't they? Well yes, they will, but only from their perspective. If it worked out well for them, they're likely to advise you to go ahead. But that's their personal biased opinion. If it didn't work out for them, they'll probably advise you the opposite. And yet you and I both know that some property investments go well and others don't, so their standpoint isn't going to be the only one.

I'm not saying don't consult them. They will probably have some useful insights. But don't think just because they have more experience than you that their advice is necessarily right. If you can find someone with a different track record, that will help to balance things. However what you have now is two personal opinions from people who have more experience than you. Neither might be right for you. Just remember that.

This brings us back to facts and whether they're biased. Assuming the facts you collect are true,\* whoever is presenting them will have chosen which facts they consider relevant, and that process contains an inherent bias. You only have to look at how political parties argue over facts to see this process taken to its logical

---

\* But obviously don't just assume it.

conclusion. Usually (although perhaps not always) both will present true facts that seem to support opposite arguments. That's because they pick different data, or present it in different ways, so it appears to say what they want it to.

You might be consulting someone who has no intention of doing this, but it's unavoidable. People have deep-seated and sometimes unconscious beliefs about things that influence their perception of the facts. Imagine asking advice about property investments from someone born into wealth and then from someone who grew up in a council house. They might well have very different values around the ethics of housing, and these are likely to be reflected in their advice. They may not realise it, but they are likely to quote the facts that back up their beliefs (see Rule 92).

Look, I'm not saying you can't ask anyone's advice. I'm just saying be aware of this stuff. A Rules player thinks about these things before asking advice and weighs them against the advice itself.

> # AN OPINION IS ALWAYS A PERSONAL STANDPOINT, AND EVERYONE HAS THEIR OWN TAKE

# Be your own advisor

Some decisions are less about facts, more about feelings. From what colour to paint the bathroom, to whether to hit send on your stinky email to your landlord, these are ultimately decisions only you can make. Of course you know that, but it's still good to get advice from other people.

Who to ask though? Maybe your mum, or perhaps your best friend. Or a work colleague, your partner, your brother . . . how are you going to choose? Well, I know how most of us choose a lot of the time.

I had a lightbulb moment about this a few years ago. I can't even remember what the decision was, but I decided to call a particular person. When I couldn't reach them, I figured I'd better call someone else. There was an obvious alternative person but I caught myself prevaricating about making the call. 'Hang on,' I thought. 'Why don't I want to call him?' I thought about this for a moment and the answer became obvious: I didn't trust him to give me the advice I wanted to hear.

Interesting. So I knew what advice I was after. I knew what my instincts were telling me already, and I was looking for someone who would agree with me. Once I'd realised this, I had my answer and I no longer needed to call anyone for advice. I could make my mind up all by myself, without help. Indeed apparently I already had.

This is a really useful insight into the workings of your own mind. It saves you from almost ever having to ask anyone else's advice on those emotional decisions. With enough self-awareness, you can become your own advisor. Now how much easier does that make things?

Hmmm. Funnily enough, it makes things slightly more confusing. Most of us *like* asking our friends for advice – albeit the friends who will say what we want to hear – so discovering that you never need ask their advice again leaves most people feeling slightly underwhelmed. What's all that about, then?

Asking advice satisfies a number of human emotional needs, and arriving at the right answer is only one of them. So long as you ask someone who is likely to give you the advice you want, the conversation will strengthen the bond between you. Moreover, when they say what you want them to, it will validate your own feelings – if you lack confidence in your decision you'll feel much better for knowing your dad, or boss, or sister agreed with you. Even if you did only ask them because you knew they would. And, of course, talking through your problems is an excuse to talk about yourself which, if we're brutally honest with ourselves, most of us enjoy.

So you don't have to stop asking people for advice now you know you don't need it. Just be honest with yourself about what your instincts are, and why you're having that conversation at all.

> ASKING ADVICE SATISFIES
> A NUMBER OF HUMAN
> EMOTIONAL NEEDS, AND
> ARRIVING AT THE RIGHT
> ANSWER IS ONLY ONE OF
> THEM

# Don't jump to conclusions

I was called in once by a company that made high-end one-off pieces of furniture to sell locally. They showed me some of it – lovely big kitchen tables, handcrafted wardrobes and armoires, solid traditional dressers. Beautiful. Their problem was that they were struggling to sell the stuff. They had discovered, somewhat late in the day, that most local people were looking for side tables and little cupboards and wall shelves, and there was almost no demand for the big luxury furniture their workshop was filling up with.

It's a pretty good example of how big a hole you can dig for yourself by making false assumptions. Want another one? I know a couple who decided they wanted to move back to the area they grew up in 40 years previously. They bought a house, got planning permission for a new build in the garden, built the new house, sold off the original house – all of which took literally years – and then realised, when they were finally able to move, that actually they didn't want to be that far away from the grandchildren and all their friends. They had just assumed they'd be happy back in their old stomping ground without thinking through that assumption.

When you consider it, most big decisions are based on a whole series of choices or mini decisions. So you might decide that you want to start your own business. Now you have to decide what sort of business, where you'll run it from, how you'll raise the funds, and so on. You'll draw up a business plan, which will entail putting together estimates of costs and income and likely sales. The problem comes when you sort of forget they were only estimates and treat them as firm figures. Or assume there's a market when there isn't – or at least not without adjusting the costs, price, or products or service you offer. You could end up ploughing all your savings into a doomed business – pretty much what my furniture makers had done.

Want to change jobs? Once you've made that decision, you'll go on to decide whether you want to stay in the industry or change careers, and then what jobs to apply for, and even whether to relocate. But hang on . . . suppose the original decision was wrong? You started at square two and assumed a new job was the answer to all your problems – a classic form of jumping to conclusions. Those early wrong assumptions are especially dangerous, because so many of your subsequent mini decisions are predicated on them.

If you don't want to make this kind of mistake, you need to ask yourself right from the start 'Why do I think this? What's my evidence for it? How do I know it's true?' Get other people's opinions as well as your own. Ask as many people as you reasonably can to interrogate your plans, cross-examine you on where you're getting your information from, query your assumptions, question why you're so sure this is the right decision. Just make sure you don't dig yourself a big deep hole through not thinking properly.

> # MOST BIG DECISIONS ARE BASED ON A WHOLE SERIES OF CHOICES OR MINI DECISIONS

# RULE 79

# Understand your emotions

Emotion certainly has a part to play in making good decisions (I'll come on to that in the next Rule).* However, emotions are the culprit in a huge number of bad decisions. My own personal fault is making snap decisions for no good reason. Frankly, how much can it matter when you're choosing which chocolate bar to buy, or which evening to go to the cinema? But it's a whole different story when you're buying a house or a car or booking an expensive holiday or deciding whether to take a job, or indeed whether to hand in your notice in a fit of pique.

If this describes you, just stop it (I'm talking to myself here too). I understand, I really do, but it's only a matter of time before you do something you really can't afford, or is entirely unfair to someone else. Look, you have to know yourself and recognise your shortcomings if you want to be a Rules thinker. And we gut decision makers have to curb our tendencies when it comes to the big decisions. If you're anything like me, deep down you know perfectly well when you're making a decision faster than is seemly. So make yourself take time out and don't act on the decision for a fixed period of time appropriate to the decision. Maybe 24 hours, maybe a month. If you don't know how long the enforced pause should be, ask advice (and not from another snap decision maker). For big or expensive decisions, also do some research. *Proper* research . . .

Ah yes, that's another problem with emotions. It's so tempting only to look for facts that support the decision your gut feeling tells you to take, or only to ask advice from the people you're confident will agree with you (as in Rule 76). Even if you're not prone

---

* Before I cover procrastination. It'll be fine to leave that a bit longer . . .

to snap decisions, most of us are susceptible to fooling ourselves. You want to buy an expensive electric car so you just research how cheap it is to run, you like the thought of working abroad so you only look into the benefits for your CV, you fancy a luxury holiday so you find one that's a bargain price for what it is.

Ooh, or you tell yourself you 'deserve it'. That's a good one. Well, maybe you do. But that's not actually a sound basis for spending money you can't spare. Do you also deserve the overdraft it could result in? It's your money, go ahead and spend it if you want to. Just be honest about whether it's a wise decision and, if it's not, make a conscious decision to spend your money unwisely. Don't kid yourself it can be justified rationally.

Now, electric cars are a good thing for the environment. Working abroad has lots of positives. Who doesn't enjoy a luxury holiday? I'm not saying any of these things are right or wrong in themselves. But are they the best decision, right now, for you? That's about much more than your emotional response. It's about your bank balance, your other commitments, your time, your family . . . so consider all the relevant factors, not only the ones that suit your emotional response. That way, if you make an irrational decision, you do it with your eyes wide open.

> **IF YOU MAKE AN IRRATIONAL DECISION, DO IT WITH YOUR EYES WIDE OPEN**

# RULE 80

# Balance logic and emotion

So it's not good to let your emotions get the better of you if you want to make the best decision. But interestingly, it's not good to remove all emotion from the exercise either.

Research has been done with people who have suffered brain damage that makes them unable to feel emotions. And one thing they all have in common is that they can't make decisions. They can rationalise all the arguments, but they don't know how to plump for a particular choice. Neuroscientists have concluded that this is because very few decisions are without any kind of emotional component. Even choosing between coffee and tea, or cereal and toast, becomes almost impossible if you can't bring your emotions into play. So where does that leave you when you're choosing a job or a house or a car, let alone whether to have children or whether to end a relationship?

There's a common fallacy that emotions are irrational, and decision making should be a rational process – therefore leaving no room for emotions. The last Rule made it very clear how it's possible for emotions to get in the way of good decisions, but so does an absence of emotion. Your feelings do several important jobs when it comes to deciding what to do.

For one thing, without any emotional input, it's very hard to know how much importance to attach to all your research and information. Does this factor outweigh that one? Is this data as relevant as that? Is it worth taking an exciting and career-enhancing job in the USA, given that you won't be able to buy Marmite there? Should you buy this perfect flat that ticks all your boxes, even though it's three floors up and there's always a possibility the lift might break down? I'm using extreme examples to make my point: without emotion, how can you balance your career against Marmite?* In the same way, how can you assess the risks accurately without any emotional input? (We'll look at risk in more detail in Rule 91 by the way.)

---

* I'm implying here that the choice should be obvious, but actually I suspect my editor would follow the Marmite. *[Yes, I would! – Ed]*

Emotion can be a key part of the overall question too. Suppose that flat ticks all the practical boxes, but you're afraid you might be lonely that far from your friends? That fear – and that potential for loneliness – are important considerations. They can't be quantified rationally either. Are you slightly anxious that you might be a bit isolated until you've made new friends or are you dreading the possibility you might be permanently unhappy? Those are answers only you can give, and only on an emotional level. And they're just as important as all the practical factors (as you'll have established by using your emotional judgement to weigh them up).

Another important reason for making decisions with an emotional ingredient is that you'll feel (yes, an emotion word) much more investment in the decision if you have considered it emotionally. You'll buy into it, be far more committed to making it work, and your approach to it will be more positive.

So you have to balance emotional and rational thinking. The crucial thing is that you are self-aware about this, and you understand the role your emotions are playing.

THERE'S A COMMON FALLACY
THAT EMOTIONS ARE
IRRATIONAL, AND DECISION
MAKING SHOULD BE A
RATIONAL PROCESS

# Learn to compromise

You can't always have what you want. My mother used to tell me that and – much as I hate to admit it – she was right. In fact, you very rarely get *exactly* what you want. Not when it matters. If you're not prepared to settle for less than perfect, you may end up with nothing at all.

A friend of mine has a mother who has been trying to move house for 15 years, but won't buy a house that doesn't tick every single box. Unfortunately she sold her last house 15 years ago, and the money sitting in the bank (from which she has to pay out rent) has not increased in value as much as house prices have risen over that time. So in fact, it becomes harder and harder to find the perfect house because her ideal house is no longer in her price range. Not unless she moves to a different area, or has fewer bedrooms, or a smaller garden . . . but all those things would require compromise.

See? If you won't compromise, it becomes ridiculously hard to make a decision at all. You need to think through the compromises you will and won't make as part of the whole exercise. If you don't, you can find yourself procrastinating* on a grand scale, like my friend's mother. Often, as in her case, there's a choice of compromises and you don't necessarily need to make all of them.

This is another area where you have to make some room for emotions. Some compromises appear to be entirely rational, but that may be misleading. Suppose you can't make your new business model work unless you reduce your costs. That sounds pretty unemotional, but actually, think about it. How can you reduce costs? Find a cheaper supplier, reduce quality, find premises in a cheaper area, don't take on as many staff and work harder yourself? I think you'll find that choosing between those compromises is going to be quite an emotional thought process.

---

\* Yeah, yeah, I'm coming to that . . . don't hassle me.

So a whole big part of good decision making is about identifying the compromises you might need to make, working out how far you'll compromise (maybe you'll change careers without a salary increase, but not if it meant a drop in salary), and then choosing between the different areas of compromise. Or balancing them against each other – a small compromise here, a bigger one there.

And well before you can take the decision, you need to know your limit. What's your bottom line – or the bottom line on each element of compromise? If you want to be happy with this decision, and with everything that flows from it in the future, what is the point you won't go beyond? As always think it all through, and understand all your reasoning, before you commit to the final decision.

IF YOU'RE NOT PREPARED
TO SETTLE FOR LESS THAN
PERFECT, YOU MAY END UP
WITH NOTHING AT ALL

# RULE 82

# Find option C

Suppose you're not happy with any of the options, but you can't sidestep the decision? Maybe a member of your team has left and you have to appoint someone new. Or perhaps you can't afford to stay in your current house and need to move. Or you and your partner are getting married but have widely different views on how many people to invite to the wedding.

These are decisions that have to be made and where you can't see a good option. They can be hugely problematic and can even feel like stalemate if you're in conflict with someone else. Making a good decision can feel exhilarating. Failing to make any decision can be miserable, depressing, fraught, frustrating and overwhelming.

So don't let it happen. This is where you have to get properly creative. If none of the options on the table will do, clearly you will have to find another option. I've noticed that the people who are best at doing this are the ones who approach it in a positive frame of mind. As Henry Ford said, 'Whether you think you can, or you think you can't – you're right.' If you believe there's another option out there, you'll find it. If you think this is it, and what's the point looking, and nothing will solve the problem, and it's all a waste of time . . . I'm willing to bet that a new and workable option will never present itself to you. Or if it does, you won't recognise it.

Let's see where we can get to with the example I started with. You've lost a team member, you've advertised and you've interviewed, and you can't find a suitable replacement. So how about advertising somewhere new and maybe unexpected? How about taking on someone less experienced than you originally wanted (so a lower salary) and investing in training them (with the money saved)? How about reallocating roles in the team so you can recruit someone with a completely different set of skills? How about just not recruiting at all? Look, that's just a fraction of the possible solutions that might exist. Not all of them will be viable, but some will, and so will others I haven't suggested.

If you can't agree a decision with someone else, getting creative can also be a way to save face. Suppose you're at a stand-off where you insist on option A and they demand option B (I know this is unlikely if you're a Rules player, but it can happen even to us occasionally). You might both privately wish it hadn't come to this, but not feel ready to capitulate. What you need is option C. Something you can both agree on without backing down from your original veto of the other one's preferred decision. So you want a small family wedding and your partner wants to invite 150 people? (I'm assuming you've both vetoed inviting 75 people and having a wedding neither of you really wants.) What if you eloped romantically? Or got married in a tropical paradise where fewer people can afford to attend but, well, you'd be in a tropical paradise, so who really cares? Or don't get married at all, at least for now – again, the possibilities are almost infinite. You just have to find the one that works.

> # IF NONE OF THE OPTIONS ON THE TABLE WILL DO, CLEARLY YOU WILL HAVE TO FIND ANOTHER OPTION

# RULE 83

## Assess the cost of a bad decision

I well remember talking to a friend once who was agonising over a tricky decision. He had been losing sleep over it, worried he might get it wrong. I asked him, 'What's the worst-case scenario?' and had the delight of watching the relief palpably spread across his face as he realised that although it was a big decision, the worst that could happen wasn't that bad.

You'd be surprised how often this is the case. In that instance, he was trying to decide whether to change jobs. He worked in an industry with a buoyant jobs market, and had valuable skills, so actually if he hated the new job he could just move again. Not ideal, but also not a catastrophe, not that likely, not worth losing sleep over.

Suppose you're moving house. If you're looking for somewhere to be for the next 20 years, where you can raise a family while commuting easily to work, you really want to get it right first time. It's still not the end of the world if you have to move again, but it's costly and stressful and time-consuming. However if you're looking for a flat on your own near a job you only plan to be in for a couple of years, it matters much less if it's not perfect. You can't properly assess which is the right decision if you don't understand the consequences of making the wrong decision.

And think long term. I've seen ostensibly bad decisions have brilliant long-term consequences. You think the job you turned down would have been so much better than the one you took, but five or ten years down the line, you could have risen higher than you ever would have otherwise. Promotions come up at the right moment, the company expands. . . these things may be hard – or even impossible – to predict, but think about them and you'll see that the 'wrong' decision now doesn't have to stay wrong for ever.

So think about the worst-case scenario and, alongside that, think about your back-up plan. That's really important. What will you do if your start-up business fails? What if you hate the new job? Suppose you don't get into the uni you really want? There are two reasons why this thought process is so useful. First, this is probably the worst-case scenario: if the business fails, can you sell off the equipment and stock and go back to your old job (or one very like it)? If that would leave you bankrupt, you might need a better Plan B to keep yourself solvent. However if that's financially viable, it's your worst case and your Plan B.

The second reason for this is that having a Plan B always makes life less stressful. I've observed it time and again. When people have a back-up option, they are so much less anxious than all those panicky people who simply have no idea what will happen or what they'll do if their Plan As don't work out.

One other common mistake here. Deciding to do nothing (not move house, not appoint an extra team member, not look for another job) is still a decision, and needs assessing alongside all the other options. Most people don't fully grasp that. Rules thinkers do.

---

# DECIDING TO DO NOTHING
# IS STILL A DECISION

---

# Regret is a waste of energy

There are few more pointless emotions than regret. It's all about feeling sad over something you did – or failed to do – in the past, so by definition there's no way you can change it. You could not think about it I suppose. If you *can* change an outcome you don't like, you will do. If you can't, regret can seem like the only option.

It's a bit self-indulgent though, isn't it? In the end, you're bound to end up feeling sorry for yourself. And who does that help? Much better to resolve not to be a regretter because, in all honesty, it makes no sense.

The fact is, you have no idea what would happen if you made a different decision. Listen, if you'd taken that job after all, that now looks so perfect through your rose-tinted glasses, perhaps you'd have been so excited on your first day that you forgot to look as you crossed the road, and got hit by a car. No, I know it's not likely, but you don't *know*. The colleague at the next desk might have been a nightmare to work with, you might have been headhunted by a client and then hated *that* job . . . each example may be unlikely, but there are infinite possibilities and the ones that actually happened might not have been nearly as good as you imagine. So it's just pointless regretting your decisions, whatever they are, because the alternative always *could* have been worse.

Even if you've gone through bad times as a result of your past decisions (which might still have been better than the alternatives, see above) well, those experiences are what made you the incredible person you are now. Without hardship or trauma or frustration or grief, we wouldn't grow into the complex and fascinating people we all are. Take those experiences away, and you have to give up part of yourself with them. So let go of the regret, and value what you've learnt and who it has made you.

There is something else you can do too – not about past regrets but to avoid future ones: make really strong decisions and make them consciously. If you think through every decision you make from now on, following these Rules and any practical strategies you can find in books or online, then you will know that each decision has been the best one you could have made at the time. You'll be able to look back and know that in the same circumstances, you would do the same thing again. You would collect the same information, consider the same options, consult the same advisors, make the same compromises, come up with the same options, set yourself the same parameters, allow your emotions the same weight, and come down in favour of the same course of action.

It's pretty hard to regret a decision that you would still make in the same situation. You may occasionally wish things had turned out differently, but you won't kick yourself for it.

---

## MAKE REALLY STRONG DECISIONS AND MAKE THEM CONSCIOUSLY

# Be honest about procrastinating

Oh, yeah, I said I'd mention procrastination at some point, didn't I? Might as well do that now I guess. Um, yes . . . I seem to have covered everything else in this section.

Best get on with it then.

Sometimes waiting to see what happens is a good call. But it has to be a deliberate, conscious choice – a decision in itself. Usually with a time limit. For example, you might decide you'll wait a year to see what business rates do, or wait six months before handing in your notice in case a likely promotion comes up. Or delay getting married until after you've found somewhere to live together.

The rest of the time, doing nothing is just an excuse for avoiding or sidestepping the decision. So why do you need an excuse? Why not just make the decision? There are lots of possible answers to that one. And you're going to have to work out which one applies to you. Be honest now, look your decision in the face and admit why you aren't getting on with it. Once you've fessed up to yourself (it's all right, no one else needs to know), you should be able to do something about it.

Maybe it's as simple as you just don't know which decision is the right one. So identify what information (factual or emotional) is missing, and go get it. Once you put in the right data, you'll get the best answer. But you know, sometimes we can't pinpoint the right decision because it actually doesn't matter – the coffee or tea question on a bigger scale – in which case toss a coin. Yes, really. It's a good strategy, especially when the decision has a strong emotional component. Just before the coin lands, you'll know whether you're hoping it's heads or tails. It's that split-second response, not the coin, that will give you your answer.

All right, you know what to do – that's not the problem – but you're putting it off because you're overwhelmed, or you just hate change. You're looking at the daunting process instead of the wonderful end result. So focus on how great it will be when the extension is built, or you've moved to New York, or you're settled in the new job. Visualise it. Think of the space, or the new friends, or the lifestyle, or the kudos, or the peace and quiet.

If you're not sure where to start, it doesn't matter. Just pick a random starting point and, well, start. The sooner you have less still to do, the sooner it will feel less daunting.

Remember the friend's mother who's been househunting for 15 years and counting? Her procrastination comes from a steadfast refusal to compromise. And look where that's got her. Be realistic about setting yourself parameters you can actually achieve.

Sometimes, if none of these reasons for procrastinating rings true, it's because there's an underlying problem we're not addressing. Maybe, deep down, you're reluctant to set a date for the wedding because you're not 100 per cent sure you want to get married. So be honest with yourself, and get to the bottom of that. Then either set a date, cancel, or postpone while you sort out your feelings.

---

**LOOK YOUR DECISION IN THE FACE AND ADMIT WHY YOU AREN'T GETTING ON WITH IT**

---

# CRITICAL
# THINKING

Your mind needs to be honed and trained to think healthily, to be organised, to make decisions, to be creative and to solve problems. And there's one last group of skills the true Rules thinker has to master. You need to be able to think critically – that's in the old-fashioned sense of criticism, which is not about being negative but simply about evaluating.

These Rules will enable you to evaluate arguments, to think logically, to form balanced and valid opinions, to make connections, to detect inconsistency. You will be able to listen to someone else's viewpoint, read an article online, or study a book, and then evaluate it, assess data, analyse statistics, and form your own intellectual view on its merits. So it follows you'll also be able to analyse and assess your own opinions, which is always fun. If you find your position on any topic is indefensible, you don't have to tell anyone, but you can quietly modify it.

Valuable as facts and information are, they're of limited use without critical thought. This is what enables you to use the facts, to exploit the information, to critique and build on your creative ideas. If you can do this, you will be far more useful to yourself and others, not to mention far more valuable to an employer.

This section is about intellectual rigour, not about emotions. So keep in mind Rules 50, 79 and 80 and others about not letting your emotions get in the way of rational thought. When it comes to analysing data, evaluating arguments, considering options, you need your rational, incisive, logical brain firmly in control.

# Read John Donne

It doesn't have to be John Donne, although I can't think why anyone wouldn't want to read him. He was a seventeenth-century English writer of poetry and sermons (you can enjoy them whether or not you share his beliefs). Perhaps his most famous line is 'no man is an island', which is part of an eloquent sermon justifying this viewpoint. He's an easy writer to read because many of his poems are short and you can dip in and out of them, or read one a day.

You want to know why you have to read Donne? Well, the thing about Donne is that not only are his writings beautiful, brilliantly crafted, moving and still relevant today, they are also thought-provoking. To appreciate them fully, you have to engage your brain. He uses paradox, irony, complex ideas, reasoned argument, to express even the most passionate feelings.

If you're going to be a top-class critical and analytical thinker, you need some decent, meaty material to practise on. You need to train your mind by wrapping your head around some complex thinking until it becomes natural for you to think the same way when required. And it's much more fun to read beautiful words expressing surprisingly up-to-date ideas, with an occasional side of humour, than it is to immerse yourself in text books or research documents or maths problems.

If you like your humour a bit more upfront, you could try watching the comedian Stewart Lee, whose stock-in-trade is deconstructing his own act as he's performing it. Again, multi-layered and thought-provoking, which is what we're after.

Of course there are lots of other writers and performers who will serve the same purpose for you. These two are particular favourites of mine, and you might like to try them at least, if only so you can see exactly what I'm on about. Then feel free to go and find other people who give you the same kind of mental workout.

Better still, once you've enjoyed the exercise on your own, find friends who will discuss the ideas with you. Indeed who will discuss any ideas with you. We spend a lot of our social conversations catching up on news about people, or discussing events or shared interests. Nothing wrong with that. But try to find people with whom you can spend at least some time debating ideas – philosophy, politics, psychology, whatever grabs you.* Not just arguing head to head and both refusing to budge though, because that's not going to help you think better.

The aim is to make your mind more nimble, more flexible, more able to leap from point to point. Plus you need to be able to think about what you're thinking while you're thinking it. It's this active detachment, this ability to analyse and critique your own thoughts, that will elevate you to the level of a really skilled Rules thinker.

> # THINK ABOUT WHAT YOU'RE THINKING WHILE YOU'RE THINKING IT

---

* It doesn't have to begin with P.

# RULE 87

# Don't be played for a fool

The world is full of people and organisations who want you to do or believe what they tell you. From advertising campaigns to fake news, we're all surrounded by manipulative information intended to push us into buying this tin of beans, listening to this music, wearing these clothes, voting for that candidate.

I don't know about you, but I don't much care for being told what to do, and even less for being told how to think. I like to make my own decisions, form my own views, thank you very much.

Then again, I do have to buy tins of beans, and wear clothes, and indeed I choose to listen to music and to vote. And some of those messages that I read or hear or see online do sound quite appealing. Maybe they really are as good as they seem – are they? How on earth do you gauge whether you're hearing fake news or being sold false promises?

By asking some pertinent questions is how. You think for yourself these days, remember, so be conscious that everyone is selling you their product, their ideas, their beliefs for a reason. You need to know what that reason is before you can decide if you want what they're pushing. So don't be a sucker, do some serious thinking before you commit yourself. Remember Rule 3? This is the critical thinking application of that Rule.

Start by asking yourself who benefits and how from the information you're being given. If you're looking at an advertisement, it's probably obvious who's behind it. But what about broader messages? Is that campaign telling you to wear a cycle helmet being funded by the health service or by helmet manufacturers? Do the people telling you how dangerous unpasteurised milk is have a political agenda? The answer doesn't necessarily invalidate the information, but it does shed more light on it.

Some people will try to fool you by giving you partial information and hoping you won't notice. My wife remembers being told years ago by a nurse that a certain percentage of pregnant women who eat soft-cooked eggs contract salmonella, which can harm the unborn child. Even if that percentage is pretty low it would probably still deter you – it's meant to. But hang on, there's relevant information missing from that data. Did you notice? Of course you did. You also need to know how *likely* it is to harm your child. If their mother contracts salmonella, how many babies are actually harmed – 1 in 10? 1 in 100,000? That has to make a big difference. You might still decide that any risk is too high, and I'm not advising you to eat soft-boiled eggs if you're pregnant – I'm advising you to think for yourself. Including questioning why this information isn't included. There might be a very good reason, but if you're serious about being a Rules thinker, you'll want to know what it is.

Keep an eye out for emotive language too. Organisations, political parties, advertisers, they do like to use emotionally charged words and images to persuade you to think their way instead of your own. Guilt trips, fear, emotional blackmail – learn to spot when they're used against you. Charities will almost always show you a picture of an *attractive* starving child, or a *cute* furry animal.* Even if it's a good cause and you choose to give to it, you should still be aware that you're being manipulated.

> # EVERYONE IS SELLING YOU THEIR PRODUCT, THEIR IDEAS, THEIR BELIEFS FOR A REASON

* I'm never sure if this is ethical – there's an interesting question to think about.

# Stand back and take in the view

A senior manager applied for a job running a big wildlife charity. The interview process was very thorough and spread over a couple of days. It involved tours and interviews and presentations and so on. She spent ages researching the requirements of the job, the structure of the charity, how they spent their money, and put together loads of evidence that she could handle a budget, manage an organisation and had the kind of management style they were looking for.

Finally she wrote her presentation. When it was drafted, she asked a friend of mine to take a look at it for her. He told me that she had set out a really clear vision for the future of the organisation and how she would make it happen . . . but nowhere had she talked about wildlife conservation. She had been so busy focusing on the day-to-day role she was applying for, she had forgotten to look at the big picture. All the people interviewing her would be involved with the charity because they cared passionately about conservation. They weren't going to appoint someone who didn't seem interested, however impressive their management credentials.

This is such an easy, classic mistake to make. You're so focused on the detail that you miss the big picture. The problem is, you'd missed the fact there even was a big picture to miss. So how are you supposed to train your thinking skills to see things you hadn't noticed you were meant to be looking for?

The answer – as with all thinking skills – is to practise. Once your mind is in the habit of looking for the bigger picture, it will automatically think it through. So look for the bigger picture in everything you do – resolve to think about it several times a day until your mind is accustomed to seeking out the wider perspective without prompting.

Why are you washing the dishes? Detailed view: to keep them clean. Bigger view: so the family stays healthy by having hygienic plates to eat from. Why are you in this meeting? Detailed view: so we can run through the plans for next week's exhibition. Bigger view: because the exhibition needs to run smoothly in order to bring in the new business that we need for the company to grow. Why does the wildlife charity need a CEO? Detailed view: so the organisation runs effectively. Bigger view: to make a big and positive impact on wildlife.

You can think about why you're reading a bedtime story to the kids, why you're running a youth club, why you're going on holiday, why you have a dog. Sometimes the answers will be a bit hazy or there may seem to be more than one reason. Don't sweat it. You don't really need to know why you have a dog, you just need to train your brain to think more effectively. You might even want to contemplate why you're doing that.

> ## LOOK FOR THE BIGGER PICTURE IN EVERYTHING YOU DO

# RULE 89

# Look for what comes next

One of the things that sets the best thinkers apart is the way they keep on thinking where other people stop. School teachers will tell you that this is a classic way to identify the brightest students, but you can learn to do it now even if you didn't do it as a child.

Don't just passively accept the information – or the ideas – you're given. See them as a starting point and not an end point. Where can you go from here? If this is true, what else might also be true? Or indeed what else has to be true? Or what follows on? Look for deductions, extrapolations, correlations, inferences.

Obviously you can't be doing this all the time. Or can you? Actually, we all do it in a small way and it's just a matter of thinking bigger. If I suggest we go to the movies, and I tell you what time the film is on, you'll use that information to work out whether you can get back home and change after work or whether you need to go straight there. If I tell you the film's running time, you'll deduce whether this is the last showing of the evening.

A friend of mine was buying a pedigree puppy. She knew you were supposed to make sure the breeder was reputable and raising the puppies indoors around people, not outside in a puppy farm. But how could you tell from a website? She soon noticed that a lot of the websites had loads of photos of the puppies indoors – sometimes as many as a thousand photos. The dodgy breeders might fake a couple of indoor pics, but they weren't going to bother with that many. So she realised she could trust the websites with loads of photos.

These are simple calculations and natural trains of thought. But you couldn't manage even this level of thinking if you weren't taking one piece of information and using it to lead you to the next. Now what you need to do is get your brain into the habit of questioning the next steps, seeing the logical progression, making predictions, whenever you read a report, or watch the news, or hear a presentation, or listen to someone air their views.

Many entrepreneurs have started successful businesses because they read or heard something that made them think, 'Hang on, if that's the case, surely people would like this or that product . . . '

Back in 2005, one car insurer made just such a leap. Everyone knows that women drivers are statistically less of a risk. And women's behaviour typically can differ from men's in other ways – for example they are likely to carry more personal possessions around with them. This was common knowledge, but only one insurer thought through the implications of this and set up a car insurance company aimed specifically at women, with lower premiums, and handbag insurance as standard.

Whether you're making a connection that explains someone's behaviour, or recognising that language similarities between two countries suggest a historic link, or noticing that people boarding the subway train all have wet umbrellas so it must be raining up top, you're actually thinking, 'Oh, I get it, so if this is the case then that must follow . . . '

---

SEE INFORMATION AS A

STARTING POINT AND NOT

AN END POINT

---

# RULE 90

# Don't bother your pretty little head

When you're trying to assess information and draw conclusions from it, one of the hardest things can be having too much data. Maybe you're researching a particular option and there's a huge amount of stuff out there, more than you could possibly want, so which do you need and which can you safely ignore? You have to be able to sift information, and you have to be sure you're getting it right so you don't discard anything you should have kept hold of.

Facts are all very well, but how do you know if they're relevant? What if they appear to conflict with each other? If you have two similar sets of data doing roughly the same job, which one should you use?

First of all, recognise that there's such a thing as too much information. If you can't see the wood for the trees, you're overloaded. If you're doing the research because you want to use it to influence someone – your boss to adopt your proposal, your partner to agree to refurbish the kitchen, your local council to construct cycle paths – a few pieces of carefully selected data will have far more effect than a daunting pile of paperwork stuffed with statistics and figures and diagrams.

The next step is to slim the information down. If you do this before you even find it, that's better still because it's so much more efficient. You could spend all day researching information and then filtering it down, or you could do the sifting first, in effect, and only spend half a day on research. I know which I'd prefer. So think: work out what data you do and don't need before you start.

Right, what you need to do is be clear and incisive about what you're trying to achieve. As with so many kinds of skilful thinking, you need a properly thought through objective. That gives you something to measure the information against so you can judge whether it's needed or not.

So you don't simply want to persuade the council to construct cycle paths. Be more specific about the aim. Do you want an agreement in principle at this stage, or are you arguing for a specific route? What will influence them – accident statistics? Costs? Attracting tourism? Keeping the locals happy? What would make them say no? Or yes? Now we're talking. Once you understand exactly what you need to demonstrate, it's much easier to see which arguments you need to use, and therefore to back up with data. No point digging out figures on the effects on tourism, for example, unless that's actually an issue.

This ability to establish what is relevant and what isn't is essential to critical thinking, not only because it saves time but also because it enables you to streamline your thinking and direct it where it's really needed.

**WORK OUT WHAT DATA YOU DO AND DON'T NEED BEFORE YOU START**

# Consider the odds

Generally speaking, we're rubbish at calculating risk. Which is a shame, considering how useful it is to know the risk when we're assessing options and making decisions. For example, if you're afraid of flying, you'll think your flight is more likely to crash than the seasoned and relaxed flyer sitting next to you thinks. You can't both be right. What's more, you'll think the flight you're on is much more likely to crash than you would have done if you were still safely on the ground. I say 'safely', but statistically you could be much less safe on the ground – if you were driving, or crossing a road, or playing rugby. You won't take that into account though.

We're all the same, and to some extent it goes with being human. In any case even experts don't always know exactly what the risks are. So I'm not suggesting that you can think your way to being perfect at calculating risk every time. However it is important to understand the pitfalls when it comes to assessing the risk of taking a particular course of action. You need to be aware of your own perception of risk, and also that of people around you who are trying to persuade you towards, or away from, a decision.

One of the critical considerations is balancing risk against gains or losses. A small risk that will, at best, bring a minimal reward and, at worst, be catastrophic is probably not worth taking. On the other hand, a significant risk might be worthwhile if it promises huge gains at the risk of minor losses. So when you're thinking through risk, take this into account.

And bear in mind that people (yes, that's you) are more inclined to take risks that promise big benefits, even if the potential losses are also significant. Also we underestimate risks that involve an activity we enjoy compared with the risk of an activity we don't. You're more likely to underestimate the risk of doing something you have control over, such as driving or skiing or running down stairs. In fact you're more likely to underestimate any risk when you're in a good mood compared with when you're feeling upset angry or scared.

Here's a risk in itself: if you don't keep your brain primed and alert, you can fail to spot risks that you should be aware of. That's especially true if you're focused on a bigger risk. So if you're worrying about your (perceived) risk of flying, you might overlook the risk of leaving your passport at home.

Keep an eye on cumulative risk too. Some decisions involve a series of potential risks – the risk of the costs increasing, the risk of crucial people leaving, the risk of it taking longer than planned, the risk of the quality falling short. If you underestimate all of these slightly, you could have significantly underestimated the risk of the whole project. And some of these may make others more likely to happen.

> # YOU NEED TO BE AWARE OF YOUR OWN PERCEPTION OF RISK

# RULE 92

## Facts are neutral

You need to avoid all the pitfalls of sloppy thinking, and that means you need to be on the lookout for them. These are the little errors that make us believe our thinking is sharper than it is. We don't want to feel smart, we want to *be* smart. We want to spot the traps so we can take avoiding action before we fall into them.

I mentioned in Rule 76 that one of the big errors of thought is believing that the facts, the data, the stats are backing up your own viewpoint. This is known as confirmation bias, when you search out information that supports your argument, or interpret the facts that you're presented with as backing you up. It's a very comfortable thing to do – it makes you right, and saves you the effort or loss of face of changing your mind. All nice and simple.

Unless you're a Rules thinker. Smart thinking isn't always comfortable or nice. Sometimes it means re-evaluating our beliefs or changing our whole approach to a subject. That's the price you pay for being a top-class thinker. No more 'nice and comfortable' for you.

Look, facts aren't interested in helping you. They don't want to back you up, support you, corroborate your thinking. They're just facts, OK? Sometimes they might happen to reinforce your point and sometimes they might refute it. That's the way they are. What you have to do is be dispassionate about working out what they mean, because they won't tell you that. It's not their job.

Suppose I survey a thousand people and I ask them what their favourite breed of dog is. Let's imagine the highest percentage of people – 8 per cent – vote for Labradors. That is a fact (in my imaginary world) and it's not trying to tell you anything. It just is.

Along comes a Labrador lover who is delighted, but not very surprised, to learn that more people favour Labradors than any other breed. That's what they always thought – of course Labradors are best. But what's this? A Labrador hater* is looking at this data and is feeling thoroughly vindicated. Just what they thought! Fewer than 10 per cent of people favour Labradors. Ninety-two per cent of people didn't put them first.

So who is right? On one level, of course, they both are. They're both reading the data correctly. But they're interpreting it very differently because they're both falling into the trap of confirmation bias. See how easy it makes things for both of them – no need to wonder if perhaps they've been wrong up to now, no need to rethink whether other people really share their views on Labradors, no need to lose face in front of other Labrador lovers (or haters – yeah, them).

Look, you have to question your interpretation of the facts, interrogate your own thinking process, if you're going to get to the truth of anything. It may not always be pleasant, but it has to be done.

> # SMART THINKING ISN'T
> # ALWAYS COMFORTABLE
> # OR NICE

---

* I know they're not really a thing. Actually I'm starting to go off my imaginary world . . .

# Don't trust statistics

Eighty-seven per cent of statistics are made up on the spot – a fact I often quote. Although sometimes I say it's 56 per cent.

You can't really understand statistics until you understand the ways in which people can manipulate them in order to get you to agree with their way of thinking. Stats are a very appealing way to back up an argument because they look deceptively like facts. It is perfectly possible to represent actual real facts in statistical form, but you should never assume that's what you're seeing until you've checked them out thoroughly. You're a serious critical thinker and you're not going to let anyone take you for a ride.

For a start, always check where the information has come from and who is paying for it. Are you confident it's neutral? What's the size of the sample – is it a survey of 10,000 people or 8 people? Who were they? If it's a poll, what questions were asked? Suppose you were asked these two questions:

- Do you believe in freedom of choice?

- Do you believe the government should prevent people drinking to excess?

I imagine more people would answer 'yes' to the first question than to the second, and yet either could be included in a survey into attitudes to alcohol – depending on what impression it wanted to give.

Here's another common manipulation of the facts. If you own a bookshop that had 10 customers last year and now has 20, you could say you'd doubled your number of customers. True, but you've only gained 10 actual customers, and for a typical bookshop I'd say you're in trouble. Similarly if you've gone from 100 to 150 customers, you could say that last year you had only two-thirds of the customers you have now, or you could say your customer base has increased by 50 per cent. Both true, but somehow they give different impressions.

Graphs and charts give those pesky statisticians even more scope to mislead you. The most obvious example of this is where the figures up the left-hand side of a graph don't start at zero. Imagine 2 columns, one showing 155 units of whatever and the other showing 160 units. They will be quite similar heights, right? Now imagine your bar chart starts, in the bottom left corner, not at 0 but at 150, so it shows only the tip of each column. Now one of them is showing 5 units and the other shows 10: double the height. This technique, and variations on it, are designed to fool you. Don't fall for it.

And one more thing – no one is going to present you with statistics that contradict their argument. So always consider, and indeed research, whether there are other stats out there that put a different perspective altogether. Oh, and which of course might also be presented in a misleading way.

> # NO ONE IS GOING TO PRESENT YOU WITH STATISTICS THAT CONTRADICT THEIR ARGUMENT

# Understand cause and effect

Sometimes someone will try to persuade you that two pieces of data are related. They'll even show you charts and graphs to prove it. And often they'll be right – but not always. As a skilled critical thinker you won't take this at face value, will you? You'll pick it apart to make sure the correlation is real.

Stage two of the argument is to reason that, if these two things correlate, there must be a causal relationship between them: one must cause the other. A genuine example of this would be that the more people smoke in a given group, the higher the incidence of lung disease will be. That's because, as we all know, smoking causes lung disease.

You might be more surprised to learn that the rate of divorce in Maine in the USA correlates closely with the amount of margarine eaten per head. That's absolutely true. But entirely coincidental. See? Just because the initial data's accurate, it doesn't mean you can extrapolate any kind of link between the two.

When two sets of data (let's call them A and B) correlate, there are four possible explanations you should consider:

- A causes B.

- B causes A.

- They're not causally related at all.

- Something else is causing both of them.

I'll give you a classic example. In the summer, sales of ice cream and cases of murder rise at a comparable rate. However, it would be a mistake to assume that either of them is causing the other. In fact an outside factor – the heat – is the explanation for both.

Suppose you establish which make and model of car is involved in fewest collisions. So if you – a man in your 20s, for the sake of argument – buy this car, you're less likely to have an accident. Ideal! So you might think. Now let me tell you that the only reason these cars are involved in fewer accidents is because they're particularly favoured by middle-aged women drivers. That's why the accident statistics favour this model.

This is another reason why you need to investigate the source of any data you're given and question who has been surveyed or taken part in trials. For a long time, it was noted that women who had fertility treatment were more likely to develop ovarian cancer and that the hormones used in the treatment could be to blame. Doctors now think it's actually the infertility itself, rather than the treatment, that is behind the statistics. Of course the research group were all specifically women undergoing treatment and that had to be taken into account.

## PICK IT APART TO MAKE SURE THE CORRELATION IS REAL

# If you can't prove it's true, that doesn't mean it isn't

Do you believe in telepathy – that some people can tell what others are thinking when they're not even in the same room?

One of the most pervasive elements of pseudo-scientific thinking is to believe a thing can't be true unless you can prove it is. Many people will tell you that, as there's no scientific proof for these things, they can't be true. But remember, there was a time when science couldn't yet prove that the earth went around the sun. Didn't stop it doing it though.

I'm not saying that I believe in telepathy. But I don't pooh-pooh it either. Sadly I don't believe in magic (I wish I did) so personally I reckon that if it's true, there is a rational scientific explanation that no one has yet found. I have had some experiences that would seem to support the argument for telepathy, but I can't prove they weren't just surprising coincidences.*

So don't get tricked into ruling things out just because there's no proof. Clearly you have to apply your intelligence here. Almost all of physics is ultimately unprovable, as physicists will tell you, and operates on the principle that once the weight of argument becomes overwhelming, scientific theories have to be assumed to be true. Also, looking outside the world of science, it's reasonable for me to assume my family love me, even though I only have their word for it.

---

* And remember, it would be a really surprising coincidence if coincidences never happened.

On the other hand, don't mistake evidence for proof. I know a few people who can quite exasperatingly mix up their own experience for proof. If you tell them that research shows, for example, that more people with brown eyes are good at maths (yes, I made that up) immediately they will try telling you that it can't be so because their friend is really good at maths and has blue eyes, so there! Or their other friend has brown eyes and is rubbish at maths.

A good thinker understands that this means zilch. The data (that I made up) didn't say *all* brown eyed people are good at maths. Nor did it say that no non brown-eyed people were good at maths. Just that being good at maths correlated more highly with brown eyes than other eye colours. One person's experience might be unexpected, but it doesn't negate all my (meticulous and hard-earned) research results. Also, many people presented with this data will tend to notice the exceptions because they stand out. So while they might immediately think of a blue-eyed friend who is maths-minded, it may actually be that if they surveyed all their friends the results would bear out my own research. If I hadn't made it up.

So don't be guilty of muddling up evidence and proof, or assuming something unproven can't be true. Keep an open mind and evaluate all the data you're given as neutrally and dispassionately as you can.

# DON'T BE GUILTY OF MUDDLING UP EVIDENCE AND PROOF

# Don't believe it just because everyone else does

If you're one of nature's conformists, always wanting to fit in with the group, you're going to find critical thinking more challenging. There's certainly nothing wrong with being a team player, one of the gang, but it's not going to make things easy for you. That's because it's really important to understand that a thing isn't automatically so just because everyone else seems to think it is. I talked about this in Rule 1 and its importance in terms of your values and beliefs.

And it's important when it comes to critical thinking too. If we all thought the same way, all followed the same logical paths, how would anyone ever have a new thought? How would Darwin have developed his theory of evolution if he just assumed everyone else was right? How would early man have thought of settling in one place and farming the land when everyone else was quite happy hunting and gathering?

The great innovators of history didn't get where they were by thinking what everyone else was thinking. You should always know the reasoning behind your beliefs, follow your train of thought through, and never rely on 'everyone says so' or 'everyone thinks that'. Assumption is just an excuse for lazy thinking, whatever your reason for assuming, and Rules thinkers are never lazy. Well, not about their thinking anyway.

Actually, as an aside, you are allowed to be lazy in your thinking just occasionally, but only on one condition: you have to know why you're being lazy and consciously decide to let yourself get away with it this once. Maybe when you're exhausted at the end of the day, or when you can't face getting into an argument with someone who never backs down (especially if you never back down too).

Of course, you'll think some things the same as everyone else – plenty of things. There are some accepted views that are pretty inarguable. For example everyone in the motor industry thinks that it matters that cars are as safe as possible. I'm happy to go along with that. However, if you work in the car industry, it's still worth being aware that this is a universal tenet that you knowingly agree with.

But I suspect most of your auto industry colleagues also assume that cars should be designed to go as fast as possible. And should have the engine at the front. And that wipers are the only way to clean a windscreen. And the middle seat in the back doesn't have to be as comfortable as the ones either side of it (I've never got my head round that). Are you quite sure you should follow all these blindly, just because everyone else does? Maybe some of them are correct, but you'll never know if you don't question the popular assumptions.

---

## ASSUMPTION IS JUST AN EXCUSE FOR LAZY THINKING

---

# Don't believe it just because you want to

I have often wondered why some people passionately believe in conspiracy theories that really don't stand up to serious inspection – or in many cases don't stand up to the most cursory investigation. Take flat-earthers for example. They have to tie the facts in knots to justify their beliefs, postulating any number of lies and conspiracies in order to shoehorn their theory into a remotely sustainable argument.

You may well be aware of Occam's razor, a strangely named scientific 'law' which states that the simplest explanation is usually the correct one. For conspiracy theorists of all kinds, however, the explanation can never be simple. Partly because if it were it would probably be true, but also I suspect because it would be no fun if it were.

I have concluded, you see, that most people who believe in improbable theories do so because they want to. Simple as that. I'm sure they wouldn't acknowledge it, because that would undermine their argument, but I've never met anyone who espoused an unlikely theory who didn't seem to enjoy it. And I have to admit, I've been tempted to get sucked in occasionally because I love a good story, and the conspiracy theories are usually far more interesting and better plotted than the rather pedestrian but disappointingly true explanations.

For most of us sceptics, the conspiracy theories look like hokum. But they are only an extreme example of something that almost all of us do from time to time – believe a thing because we want to, rather than because rational argument tells us it is true.

We want to believe social media is good for us, we want to believe the political party we support is better than the others, we want to believe our partner isn't cheating on us, we want to believe there's a market for our product, we want to believe the dog doesn't fancy a walk today. It doesn't matter how much evidence may be piled up against us, we remain blinkered to it, and only see the few crumbs of evidence that support our theory, the theory we want to believe in.

Listen, the thoughts and beliefs and ideas you most need to question in yourself are the ones that you like, the ones that you want to hold, the ones that serve your interests in some way.

As soon as you recognise that you are thinking what you want to think, that's the signal that you need to scrutinise your beliefs and opinions extra thoroughly, and with double helpings of honesty and self-appraisal.

> THE THOUGHTS AND BELIEFS
> AND IDEAS YOU MOST NEED
> TO QUESTION IN YOURSELF
> ARE THE ONES THAT YOU LIKE

# RULE 98

# Be devil's advocate

However much you want to think critically, to believe things for the best reasons, to consider all the facts, to avoid being fooled by statistics or by too much information or confirmation bias, how can you be sure your thinking is as good as it can be? What if you truly think you're persuaded by the arguments but actually you're being swayed unconsciously by what you want to believe?

The answer is to pretend you're someone else. Someone who holds a different, opposing view from your own. Go on, have a good argument. Pick holes in your idea or belief, find the loopholes, highlight the weak points. Imagine your own views are held by someone you dislike and you'd hate to agree with them so go on, take them apart, make them feel small, show them how ludicrous their viewpoint is, force them to admit they're wrong.

OK, it is actually you. But you need to challenge your own views and opinions, your interpretation of the data, your recommendations. You need to be sure that what you think really stands up to scrutiny, in order to justify thinking it. What's more, you need to make sure it stands up to scrutiny if someone else tries to argue with it. Even if you don't change your mind, you'll find further arguments in your favour which will leave you better prepared when you're next challenged.

So imagine someone you'd like to defeat in an argument taking your original view while you put forward the counter-arguments. Try doing it out loud and playing both parts (maybe not in public – you don't want to get arrested for brawling with yourself in the street).

You could reward yourself if you manage to change your mind, although I'd like to think that by this stage of testing an argument you'll more often reassure yourself that you're right than successfully change your viewpoint. Nevertheless, you should start to worry if over time you never shift your views when you do this – there ought to be times when it makes you modify your view if you're doing it properly. U-turns are less likely and may rarely if ever happen. But you should chalk up a successfully argued U-turn as a major success for the process as a whole, not a negative reflection on your previous standpoint – which was, after all, only a midway point as it turns out.

There's one more advantage to playing devil's advocate, which is that it broadens your ability to see another person's viewpoint. The strength of being able to see both sides of an argument is hard to exaggerate as a life skill. It makes you more empathetic as well as being a far better thinker. So the devil's advocate approach to testing your own ideas is not only valuable when it comes to the immediate thought in hand, but also for the way it develops your thinking as a whole.

# GO ON, HAVE A GOOD
# ARGUMENT

# Don't go into lockdown

What happens to your beliefs when information changes or prevailing views shift? Do you change your mind or do you accommodate it? Or do you stick with what you always thought – it was good enough then so it's good enough now?

That's the attitude a lot of people take, but it simply makes no sense. We know people generally dislike change, at least when they're not in control of it. But look, the whole of scientific progress relies on modifying or even scrapping theories when new data comes along that overrides it. Newton's theory of gravity was good enough until Einstein pointed out that it only went so far.

And it's not just science this applies to. Take social attitudes. When I was young, western attitudes to race, sexuality, women were very different from what they are now. If everyone insisted on sticking with the prejudices they grew up with, things would change even more slowly than they do. And not because the idea everyone first thought of was unassailably right. The reason society's outlook has changed is not only because the younger generation takes a more egalitarian view, but because many older people also adjusted their thinking as they went along. They were persuaded by the arguments they heard and the attitudes they witnessed and the people they met, and were broad-minded enough to recognise that their old ways of thinking were out of date. Shame even more of them didn't join in.

Social attitudes change very gradually. And unless things are going at such a slow rate you hardly notice your ideas changing, most people tend not to change their minds once they're set. I'm not just talking about long-term attitudes, but about supporting more immediate arguments. Once you've decided that you definitely need to move house, or launch this product line, or set up a local women's football team, or become vegan, or drop your prices, it's easy to fix that belief in your mind. You may have considered it closely when you were still deciding, but now you close off your thinking. It's a done deal. Time to stop thinking, lock down your decision and get on with it.

Um . . . who said you have to stop thinking just because you're doing? These kinds of ideas shouldn't be set in stone. That makes no sense. If new information comes along, why wouldn't you reconsider – and perhaps revise – your view? People used to think smoking was good for you, especially if your lungs were bad (which they very possibly were if you smoked). Then scientists produced new information to show that actually smoking was very unhealthy. Do you think existing smokers should have ignored this new information? Of course you don't.

You decide to move house. Now suppose you take a big financial hit, or your adult son wants to move back in with you, or the housing market changes unexpectedly. It only makes sense to reconsider your decision. You might stick with it or you might not, but you need to be open to change. So never be sure of anything – or at least only until new information comes along. Then double-check whether your view is still valid.

> WHO SAID YOU HAVE
> TO STOP THINKING JUST
> BECAUSE YOU'RE DOING?

# Opinions aren't facts

I know I said in the introduction to this section that there's no place for emotion in critical thinking. However I should point out that a lot of 'rational' arguments are in fact emotional and not rational at all. You need to be able to identify them, whether it's your own view or someone else's.

Here in the UK, the argument over whether we should be part of the European Union has been raging for about half a century. At any stage – do we join, do we leave, do we sign this or that treaty – people on both sides of the debate put forward their arguments passionately. You would have thought, wouldn't you, that by now the country would have worked out which was the right answer. Where the weight of argument fell. But they haven't (and they probably never will).

And why haven't they? Simple. It's because there isn't a right or wrong answer. No one ever really knows what will happen to the economy, immigration, industry until they get there. It's all forecasts and what ifs and worst-case scenarios. All those people who claim the facts support their argument are kidding themselves. If the facts coherently supported one argument over the other, we'd pretty much all be persuaded.

What all these people have is an opinion. A belief that is driven by their hearts, not their heads. They *want* to be part of a bigger Europe, or they *feel* that immigration is bad for the country, or they *believe in* devolving power to the most local level possible. All of these beliefs are quite understandable, but unfortunately they're not all compatible with each other, which is why there's no agreement. Everyone can find examples and data and arguments that support their case, and apparently everyone can also ignore examples and data and arguments that don't.

This is the reason why it's said you should never discuss politics or religion because it always leads to arguments. People won't change their minds on these points through rational argument, because they're not rational standpoints. They're valid beliefs, but they weren't arrived at through logical reasoning and they're not going to give way to it. Nevertheless people like to debate them as if they were rational and can get extremely heated when they have to defend their non-rational position against a set of facts and statistics that may offer a serious challenge.

I'm not sure why people aren't more aware of this, and why they feel it's not acceptable to say, 'I'm not interested in logical argument thank you. This is what I believe in my heart and I don't feel the need to defend it rationally. It's not based on fact but on my personal values.'

Actually what we do, though, is to take a position based on our values, and then post-rationalise it with what we consider to be logical reasoning, using whatever facts and examples happen to support us.

It's fine to hold these non-rational beliefs, but be self-aware about it. Recognise when other people are doing it (less wittingly* than you), and realise that you can never defeat them in an argument because that's not how it works. Argue if you want to, but accept it will get you nowhere.

> # THEY'RE VALID BELIEFS, BUT THEY WEREN'T ARRIVED AT THROUGH LOGICAL REASONING

---

* Is that a word? It should be a word.

# THESE ARE THE RULES

This collection of Rules of Thinking joins the other titles in the series in setting out guidelines for various aspects of our lives. These are not commandments, no one is telling you that you *must* live this way. They are simply observations about the habits, attitudes and practices that happier, more successful people live by. So it follows that, if we adopt them ourselves, we too will be happier and more successful. They're not compulsory, but why wouldn't you want to join in?

# How to use the Rules

It can be a bit daunting to read a book with 100 Rules for a happier more successful life. I mean, where do you start? You'll probably find you follow a few of them already, but how can you be expected to learn dozens of new Rules all at once and start putting them all into practice? Don't panic, you don't have to. Remember, you don't *have* to do anything – you're doing this because you want to. Let's keep it at a manageable level so you go on wanting to.

You can go about this any way you like, but if you want advice, here's what I recommend. Go through the book and pick out three or four Rules that you feel would make a big difference to you, or that jumped out at you when you first read them, or that seem like a good starting point for you. Write them down here:

Just work on these for a couple of weeks until they've become ingrained and you don't have to try so hard with them. They've become a habit. Great stuff, well done. Now you can repeat the exercise with a few more Rules you'd like to tackle next. Write them here:

Excellent. Now you're really making progress. Keep working through the Rules at your own pace – there's no rush. And remember, I'm not the only one who can observe other people and see what works for them that could work for me too. So when you identify a Rule I haven't included here, you can include it yourself. Keep a list of additional Rules you want to emulate and write them down:

It seems a shame to keep these new Rules to yourself, so please feel free to share them with other people. If you'd like to share them on my Facebook page I'd love to hear from you: www.facebook.com/richardtemplar.